A BACKPACK, A CHAIR AND A BEARD

The True Story of an
Incredible Journey

EAMON WOOD

The Wayward Wheeler

First Published 2020
By Eamon Wood

© Copyright 2020
All rights reserved.

ISBN 978-0-473-54514-7 (Soft cover)
ISBN 978-0-473-55054-7 (Epub)
ISBN 978-0-473-55055-4 (Kindle)

Except for the purpose of fair reviewing, no part of this publication may be reproduced or transmitted in any form or by any means, electronic or mechanical, including photocopying, recording or any information storage and retrieval system, without the prior written permission from the publisher.

The Copy Press, Nelson, New Zealand
www.copypress.co.nz

CONTENTS

A Note From the Author 1

Prologue 4

An Accidental Family ... and a Family Accident 7

My Tumultuous Teens 16

At Home in My Body 19

The Saving Grace of Sport 22

Seduced by Alcohol 26

The Thought 29

The Test 34

The Adventure: New Zealand 39

    Taking the first step 39

    Fox Glacier 56

    Lake Wanaka 57

    Going The Wrong Way 61

    Arrowtown and Kinloch 63

    Rolling into a New Year 69

    Back to Christchurch ... But Not for Long 74

    Outward Bound, Anakiwa 78

    Raetihi Bay: Grandad and Nan 82

The Goodbye … and The Start 93
    Sandwich, Kent 99
    Brighton 101
    London 114
    Hitting the Road 119
    Oban, Scotland 120

Starting a New Chapter in America 126
    Newark, New Jersey 127
    Philadelphia, Pennsylvania 130
    Locust Gap, Pennsylvania 135
    Saint Augustine, Florida 137
    Key West, Florida 143
    160 Miles of Freedom 145
    Lafayette, Louisiana 154
    Austin, Texas 159
    New York, New York 166

Postcards from Europe 173
    Where There Was One, Now There Were Two 174
    You're an Inspiration 178
    Your Instincts are Smarter Than You 181
    Freefalling into Freedom 185
    Friends are Worth the Time 192
    Naked Culture Shock 193
    The Wrong Way is Sometimes The Right Way 195
    Two Weeks in the Smallest Mobile Home 197

A Hard Decision 198
I Might Not Have Limits, But My Wheelchair Does 205
It's Okay to Explore on Your Own 208
On the Brink of the Journey Home 210
The Last Leg: Back to Spain 211
The Journey Ends 214
Catching Some Shut-eye in Hong Kong 215

Home to Reflect 218
Epilogue … Three Years On 220

A NOTE FROM THE AUTHOR

DO YOU REMEMBER what you were thinking at 22? For some of you, that was a long time ago, and for some of you, that is the now.

At 22—which wasn't that long ago—I had a thought. A big, daring, scary, life-changing thought. It was the kind of idea that would change me forever; shape my destiny, direct my life's purpose, and redefine my perception of who I am, what I'm capable of, and what I want to do with my life.

I was going to tour the world … well, at least as much of Europe and the United States as I could. Not the fancy, four-star-hotel-and restaurant tours of everyone's fantasies, the kind we see on TV, the kind that pops up in your feed and makes you stop and daydream. I was going to be roughing it, travelling from city to city with very little money, sleeping wherever I could lay my head, eating whenever I got the chance, and soaking in the marvels of some of the western world's oldest and most culture-soaked cities. I was going to meet people, swap stories, and share points of view, so that we would both come away the richer after each encounter.

It was going to be just my backpack, my beard, my wheelchair, and me.

BUT FIRST, LET'S WIND BACK THE CLOCK A BIT. I'm ten years old, in my family's house bus, which is just planted on a hillside in the middle of my native New Zealand bush. I'm looking at a cake with little love hearts around the edges. This is my earliest moment of total self-awareness. I became completely conscious of where I was, in the context of the vastness that stretched out around me: the New Zealand bush extending as far out as I could see, down into the valley, on and on to the hazy grey-blue mountains. Something had sparked in me as I made a wish to be able to walk again, just as I had wished every birthday for the last five years—a drive, a feeling of expansion of some kind that something was missing. For whatever reason, that was when I started to want more for myself. To become more.

Here I am … to tell a story. Not so much about my life, but more about an adventure—one of many that I have had over my short existence so far… a story of how at twenty-two I had a thought.

PROLOGUE

Iona, Scotland

I COULD SEE THE SMALL ISLAND of Iona from when I got on the ferry, which cost just three pounds or something equally ridiculous. There only seemed to be two roads, so I wheeled down the one that looked more promising. It felt like this isle was as far from the other end of the earth as I could possibly go.

The lack of noise and the constant sound of the ocean breeze filled up my senses. At the end of the road there was a sign which said IONA HOSTEL: VOTED BEST ECO-HOSTEL IN SCOTLAND. Well, firstly, I was surprised that there was a hostel at the end of the earth, and, secondly, I couldn't see it. Was being invisible also good for the environment?

Turned out it was hidden behind and down a grassy hill. I went down and waved to a woman who was at the door. She explained she was a volunteer there and showed

me around. I said thanks. The fee was just 20 pounds a night, which, in the grand scheme of things, wasn't super expensive, but I had money on my mind.

I thought I'd just catch the ferry back to Mull and sleep in the car there instead, because Mull was nice too. As I made my way out of the entrance to the hostel, I noticed a gate leading to a grassy field. The ground was cushiony soft and the track ran through a mountainous field of what felt like total freedom—the sound of the ocean and the soft breeze looking out from this island left me feeling like I had it all to myself at the end of the earth. This is what I'd envisioned my dream of peace to be, even as far back as that life-changing day when I'd first seen the Durdle Door on TV. I just lay there, looking up and out. It was so peaceful … this was why I was travelling.

How could I not stay after that peaceful moment? I wheeled back down to the hostel and checked in. Then I wheeled down to the beach, parked up, jumped down onto the grass and spent the next hour or so watching the sunset, listening to the ocean and soaking it all in. Just being. After days of driving and taking ferries, here I was, wheeling around on this tiny isle of Iona! Everything was worth this moment.

AN ACCIDENTAL FAMILY ... AND A FAMILY ACCIDENT

MY MOTHER, KIM, WAS A FREE SPIRIT. She called herself Rosa, wore brightly coloured, flowing gypsy dresses, and believed in the power of crystals. She hugged everyone—when her mood was good.

She had me when she was just 19, after having conceived me during a one-night stand while on a visit to England. She never told me the name of my birth father.

As a child, I understood that she was an alcoholic, but for me it didn't seem strange. She was who she was. At heart a sweet person; I just saw her as a bit crazy. When I was a few months old she began a relationship with the man who I call Dad, Geoff. They eventually had two more children: my brother, Malachy, and my sister, Faith.

Mum was impulsive, and her spontaneity sometimes had consequences. I remember one time she and Dad were having an argument while we were all crammed into his van. She just opened the door and bailed, launching herself onto the tarmac that was speeding past under our wheels.

We didn't feel unsafe; she was a good mum and gave us what we needed; food, clothes, schooling. But sometimes, the craziness got to be too much. Malachy, Faith and I once plotted to run away, but our ambitions were stillborn, as we realised we had nowhere to run to.

I was four and a half years old when I lost the use of my legs. Mum and I were heading home from an early morning party. It was daylight. I've no way of knowing whether she'd been drinking or not, but given what I grew to know about her, it was likely. She was just 24.

At some point during that drive, she fell asleep at the wheel. We were somewhere between Motueka and Nelson, alongside an inlet to the Tasman Sea. Lucky for me, the tide was out.

I was snugly belted in, with one of those across-the-lap seatbelts you don't see around much anymore—with good reason. I felt warm and cosy, enjoying the fact that it was just the two of us; me and my mum.

I remember the feel of the car careening off the side of the road, down an embankment and onto stony ground. I remember standing up—how I got free of the seatbelt, I have no idea. Then I remember falling down.

The accident

I woke up some time later, surrounded by people who were all staring down at me. After that, it's just a blur. Tools that had been lying idle in the back of the car had been launched at me, fortunately missing my head, but tearing into my shoulder. I still have the scars to prove it. My mother suffered a broken ankle.

My diagnosis wasn't great. My lap belt had held only too well, causing traumatic injury to my spinal cord in the region of T12 L1. My spinal cord was stretched rather than severed, so I'm considered an incomplete paraplegic. I haven't fully lost sensation and can still move my legs. From the knees down, however, there's only a dull tingle, the kind you feel when you've been numbed up by the dentist. I have sensation and fairly good mobility, so I'm grateful for that.

Every year I go back to the spinal clinic where I was first treated, where I even see nurses who'd been there 26 years ago when I was first brought in. They run routine checks on my spinal injury, kidneys, and bladder. They reminisce about me at age four, wheeling myself up and down the halls on a skateboard during my months of recuperation. Calling to them to watch me go. Happy and laughing, a normal kid.

Mum never said anything about it to me, although I guess guilt must have added fuel to the fire of her alcoholism. But I've never held it against her, never said a bitter word. The idea that she was to blame … I let it go.

MY BOY DAYS WERE, for the most part, happy. Since I was injured at such a young age, I was never more than vaguely aware that I was different. The way I got around was normal, and my siblings never treated me otherwise. Malachy and I would brawl, wrestle and play as any pair of brothers would. If he was going down a hill, I was going down with him. He'd help me if I was stuck, whether he was angry with me or not, and even when he took my wheelchair away as a prank, he'd always give it back when I asked.

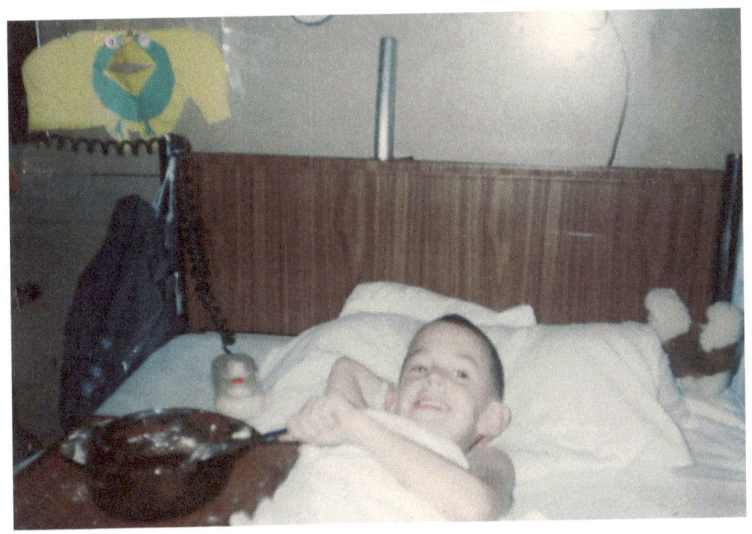

Spending my 5th birthday in the spinal unit

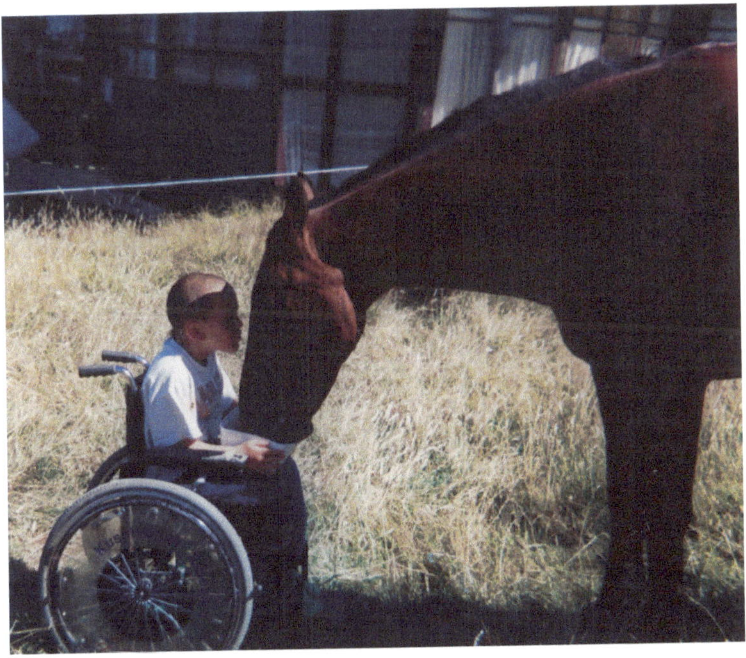

Giving Bud a kiss

Malachy and I just being normal kids climbing trees

Dad dragging me into the water in the Marlborough Sounds in winter

My parents let me be, not coddling me or making me feel there were too many things I couldn't do. If I wanted to climb a tree with the others, I just had to find a way to haul myself up. They never let me get away with thinking I was entitled to special treatment.

I've for sure taken a few tumbles, but nothing that would leave me thinking, *Boy, I wouldn't want to do that again!* Like any other active kid I've gotten a few scratches or bruises, but thankfully, never anything more serious, other than the predictable sports injuries.

I've had several surgeries over the years, most recently to straighten my legs and hips. It's especially critical when you have your accident as a child, because as you grow, your limbs can become more contracted, especially if you aren't always stretching them. It was getting harder for me to straighten my body, even lying down.

During one of my operations they broke my femurs and pelvis (yes, ouch), and re-set them so I can now stretch myself out when lying down. This means there's metal in my legs, making it even harder for them to float, even if I try ... so I swim using the power of my arms.

I've also had my Achilles tendon cut, giving me more flexibility in my ankles. I'm covered with scars which, hopefully, the ladies think are dashing!

Mum and Geoff got married a couple years after my brother and sister were born, in a small ceremony with just us running around. Although they separated, they never divorced. Geoff went on to have twin daughters, Shadow and Kiera, who are now 12. While I love them and do feel a connection, Malachy and Faith were the siblings I grew up with, the ones who rampaged around in the bush with me on sunny days, and who I watched TV with, ate with, and fought with.

While we share a blood relation, I look and feel different from them. The unanswered questions about my birth father—who he is, what he does, and what the rest of my unknown family is like—still roll around in my mind. But for Geoff, I was always his son, and his children are, to me, all my siblings.

In 2019 I took a DNA ancestry test, curious to fill the vague, shadowy void in my identity. They located a cousin on my birth father's side, and I reached out to him. I haven't heard back; a pity, because I'm curious about whether it would tell me anything about the nature vs. nurture question.

MY MOTHER DIED when I was 23, from internal haemorrhaging associated with acute liver disease. Her health condition was so severe, in fact, that although she'd been convicted of drink-driving—one of several such convictions—an empathetic judge decided not to sentence her to prison, but rather to eight months of home detention. He reasoned that, through her chronic alcoholism and frequent run-ins with the law because of her habit of drinking while driving, she had, in his words, given herself a life sentence. She spent the last few months of her life in chronic pain.

I felt oddly disconnected from her illness and death, but then, I'd felt disconnected for a long time. The burden of puberty had been heavy on my shoulders, and having to watch her sink deeper and deeper into alcoholism had made it harder, so I withdrew. I couldn't understand why she couldn't stop.

When the news came that her body was shutting down, I went to see her at her home in Blenheim, during her house arrest. I wouldn't consider it "making peace", but I was able to talk to her. She didn't have any dying wishes or regrets that she shared, but during our conversation I was able to let go and things between us. I no longer wrestled with the unanswerable question of why she kept on drinking even though it was destroying everything around her. Even though she knew it was killing her. When the visit was over, I felt better about our relationship than I had in a while. Mum passed away just a year after Faith did in a car accident; a hard blow for any family.

MY TUMULTUOUS TEENS

IF YOU ASK ME WHERE I'M "FROM", it would be a tough question to answer. I was born in Nelson City, way up to the top of New Zealand's South Island, but there is not where I stayed. My family moved about 23 times before I was 14, largely because of a vague restlessness my parents felt.

At one point I lived in a house bus in a clearing, giving me a big rocky hill to push up and down, and two acres of thick native bush, ferns, pongas, tall rimu trees and moist greenery in which to crawl around and play with the others. There was nothing else nearby; no houses, towns or any humanity.

Dad was a labourer; he did anything with his hands that paid: truck driving, farming, construction. I don't remember my mum working at all. Many times, we survived off social welfare, courtesy of the government.

At 14 I moved out, into the arms of a foster family in

Christchurch, four hours away from Nelson, through the Southern Alps. I was welcomed by a lovely woman called Karen, and her two children, John and Gemma. Gemma was my age, an able-bodied member of the basketball team I was playing on at the time, who'd offered to take me in when she saw that living at home wasn't working for me. John was a bit younger.

Karen quickly became a second mother to me. I think it was possibly strange having a 14-year-old kid come into your family, but they never treated me as an outsider. She stood by me through my reckless teenage years, and I will always be grateful to her for that. As an adult, I speak to her more often than I do even with Dad. She sends me socks for Christmas, and is always giving me some money for my birthday, despite my protests. I stay in contact with Gemma and John, and we treat each other like family.

I didn't leave home because there was direct conflict with my folks; it was just that finding common ground was a struggle. I was tired of the constant moving, especially since I had to change high schools with almost every move. And although now, as an adult, I find Greymouth quite relaxing, as a teenager it felt stifling and dreadfully dull. I constantly burned with the urge to do more, and achieve … something.

What was so reckless about those years, you ask? Well,

let me give you an example: when I was 18 my friends and I took it into our heads to go on a road trip, driving around the South Island for two weeks … only, I didn't tell anyone.

My foster family had called the police, and people were looking for me; yet there I was, waltzing back home—as much as one could waltz anywhere in a wheelchair—as if nothing had happened.

Like any teen, I'd been too wrapped up in myself to recognise that there were other beings in the universe. The realisation that someone cared enough to be worried about me, and the idea that I should have said something before I left, came as a shock.

Surprisingly, not long after that, I moved into a flat with some friends I'd gone to school with and we somehow found a way to survive.

AT HOME IN MY BODY

IN A WAY, I'M GRATEFUL that I had my accident as a child, because I grew up with the understanding that this was my new normal, and so there was no long, frustrating period of readjustment. I know what I can and can't do, and there isn't much I haven't already tried.

I have full upper body strength, enhanced by regular workouts and, of course, the exercise I get from pushing myself everywhere I want to go. Using a wheelchair might be a bit faster and easier than walking, but pushing uphill takes skill. Depending on the steepness of the hill and the depth of my motivation, I can push straight up, relying on the powerful upper body I've developed over the years through sports. If it's breakneck steep, I zig-zag up, like a sailboat tacking across the bay.

I problem-solve my way into solutions. In spaces where a wheelchair just doesn't work, I can crawl. I rarely use crutches. They're slow and cumbersome, so I resort to them on a needs-only basis.

Stairs are a challenge for me, but even they aren't unsurmountable. While I'd obviously prefer to use ramps or lifts, when I need to, I've got no problem getting out of my chair and scooting upstairs on my bum, dragging my chair behind me. I'm not crazy about doing it in public, because curious stares can burn, but it's good to know I'm never stuck.

I hate that staring. It's always at the back of my mind, this subtle, whispered anxiety that other people are watching me, especially when I've hit a rough spot, like a wheel jammed into a rut, or an awkward transition from a lower level to a higher one. It's like that cold dread you get after watching a horror movie, wondering if some shadowy entity isn't standing over your shoulder, just out of sight.

I hate the feeling that gives me, as though I'm incapable. It hurts my pride; and I often have the feeling that I'm being stared at, even when I'm not. Everyone wants to fit in.

A lot of the time, I realise that dread is in my head. Most people are briefly curious; they glance at me for half a second and then go about their business. Sometimes I get sharp looks from older folks, who belong to a generation when disabled people were kept indoors, safely out of sight and out of mind. You can't judge people for the time they grew up in, though, so I shrug that off.

Fortunately, I've never experienced disgusted looks or snide remarks. A few off-colour jokes from close friends, maybe, but that's all part of it, and I don't mind.

Worse than the stares, though, is the condescension, the patronising way some people assume that I'm mentally handicapped into the bargain. More than once strangers have addressed themselves to the people I'm with rather than asking me directly. Waiters talking over my head, asking my companion, girlfriends, parents what I'd like to eat. When that happens, I intervene and speak for myself. Not to be snarky, mind, but to give them a gentle shift in their reality.

But for the most part, people are genuinely nice and want to help. As a teen I said, "No, thank you," as a matter of course, but in my late 20s it finally dawned on me that people feel good when they help someone else.

It amuses me when people come up to me and say things like, "It's good to see you out and about," because so many disabled people become shut-ins for a variety of reasons. But I've been out and about from day one.

THE SAVING GRACE OF SPORT

APART FROM TAKING IN the occasional World Cup football match or One Day International cricket game on the television, the rest of my family wasn't into sports. That is, besides Malachy, who did a bit of skateboarding and rugby.

For me, sport has always been life-defining; it energises me, calms me, frees me. It brings my life into balance, and keeps me both mentally and physically healthy. Being in a wheelchair, there's always the tendency to be less active, and while as a young man that may not seem to be much of a problem, I'm well aware that as I grow older, maintaining my physical fitness and flexibility will become more crucial. So I keep active not just because my present self thrives on it, but because I have a responsibility to my future self.

I got involved in sport from a young age. Although I did play tennis for a while, I was irresistibly drawn to basketball. I like the team element, especially because it allowed me to interact with kids my age. I was exposed to other disabled people, and finding that common bond, that sense of belonging, was good for my self-esteem and personal development. Basketball taught me about discipline, focus and sacrifice. It's also one of the more exciting sports to play from a wheelchair.

My basketball wheelchair, by the way, is different from my everyday chair, with cambered wheels that allow for swift, sharp turns. It has extra bars for reinforcement and is more stable—so no tipping over! On the court, it's an engineering marvel, but off the court, it becomes cumbersome. Try squeezing through doorways with it; I dare you! It's also too heavy to drag upstairs, and it would be a pain to keep changing wheels and bearings. So when I'm not playing it stays where it belongs: in storage.

I also have a hand cycle that I use quite often in New Zealand; it's great for overall fitness. It's quite fast, and I enjoy being able to keep up with my friends on bikes … I might even outstrip them, if they're on a mountain bike; I've been known to hit 30 kmph!

But back to basketball. By the time I was 15 or 16, I'd gained a place on the Canterbury regional team. Although it was a wheelchair team, we often had able-bodied athletes join in, including, if you remember, Karen's daughter. Did those who played on legs have any advantage over us, who played on wheels? I don't think so. It's a game of speed, strategy and skill, and we did okay.

I made it to the national under-20s team, and was very proud of that achievement. I enjoyed training with top athletes, and my hard work was rewarded with the opportunity to travel overseas to represent my country. Visiting places like Australia, Thailand, and Korea broadened my vision and helped my soul to grow. Although New Zealand hasn't yet qualified for the Paralympics, it was an honour to make it to the qualifiers. I played on the national team for twelve years.

Although my family would drop me to my games, for a long time I didn't invite any of my friends to watch me play. I struggled with my own awkwardness, feeling vaguely embarrassed at the idea that they might be watching me zoom around in my chair, sweating and pushing my body to its limit. Did they think I looked handicapped? Did they feel sorry for me? I didn't want those nagging thoughts to fracture my focus and throw me off my game.

My sport was part of what I thought of as my "disabled life" and it was only when a given relationship achieved a certain level of trust that I was able to let them see that exposed and vulnerable part of me.

Despite this discomfort, I can't express how grateful I am that sport has come into my life. It's taken me in directions I'd never even imagined for myself, and helped shape my destiny.

At the time of writing, I'm in Germany, studying the language and playing professionally on a German league team, the Iguanas. Once again, my love for the sport has opened doors for me, allowing me to meet and mingle with like-minded people, and to roam far and wide, exploring the world and absorbing different cultures. And while most professional athletic careers don't have much of a life span, disabled sports aren't as limited, because you don't have to worry about your knees giving away. I hope to be playing well into my 40s.

SEDUCED BY ALCOHOL

I HAD MY FIRST ALCOHOLIC DRINK at 17, and, let me tell you, I went all in. It was an informal beach party on Guy Fawkes Night; me and a handful of school friends. Fireworks were going off all around us, and across the country, the obligatory bonfires were blazing. Celebrations were in full swing and the merrymaking was infectious.

There was something in a bottle. I tried it and I liked it—very much. I'd been going through a heavy time, about what, I can't recall. Teenage stuff, I guess. The wonderful burning liquid relaxed me. Soon, I stopped worrying about what people thought.

Somehow, I found myself out of my chair and in the sand, rolling around in glee. I was laughing. The others were laughing. Maybe at me and my antics, maybe just because they were as happy or as drunk as me.

I woke up on my friend's wooden deck in the early

light, damp and sandy. Because of the nerve damage I suffered, I often have to pee; but alcohol removes the level of consciousness you need to hightail it to the toilet in time. Let's just say I was forced to go home wearing my friend's clothes.

They later filled me in on all the crazy stuff I'd done, and how funny everyone thought I was. I won't lie; I enjoyed the idea of being the fun guy. In the days that followed, I veered wildly between guilt and delight. I'd discovered something that freed me from worry and sadness. I didn't need to agonise over what everyone thought about me. I could be as silly as I wanted because others around me were being silly, too. It wasn't long before I had another drink.

Don't look at me like that; I was a young man, always seeking out a party, glad to be a part of the crowd. But I, I took it past the limit. I could tell you a hundred stories about me drinking myself into a dangerous situation. Like getting blackout drunk—it doesn't take much to get me that way—and then rolling myself towards the road. Some instinct for self-preservation must have jolted me back to awareness. I came to just in time, grabbed my wheel and spun out of the way before I became a statistic. And, no, it didn't teach me a lesson. Like I said, I have a hundred stories like that to tell.

It wasn't that I was drinking alone in my room, morose

and self-destructive. It was more about enjoying parties on the weekends. It was about dancing and meeting up with friends. About being a more outgoing version of myself, that everyone liked and liked being with. Who wouldn't like drunk Eamon better than sober Eamon?

I was part of a binge culture; work all week and then eat, drink and be merry on the weekends. And being part of that binge culture, I know that when I drink it's always to excess.

I'd go through periods where I stop for a while, maybe a few months. Training with a hangover was hell, so I was focused enough not to drink much before a tournament. But I never really thought of myself as an alcoholic.

I do think back to my mother often, and her fatal attraction to alcohol, and I toy with the possibility that it may be an inherited trait. Sins of the mothers, and all that. I'm relieved that I'm more fortunate than she was, having many outlets other than alcohol. I have my sport, my wanderlust, my relationships and my friends, all of them holding me back from the brink. I know that drink is and will always be a challenge for me, and I'm proud to say that I've developed strategies to manage it.

THE THOUGHT

IT WAS RIGHT AFTER ONE OF THESE DRINKING BINGES that I first had The Thought. To be honest, if I lived another 150 years, I don't think it would have come at a harder time in my life.

I was 22, still dealing with the echoes of the deaths of my mother and sister. I'd come to realise that my flirtations with alcohol were evolving—or devolving—into an abusive relationship, and I was the one taking a beating. When you're that age, it's all too easy to hide the fact that you're struggling with alcoholism; after all, everyone's out there having a good time. Drinks were (sort of) cheap, and there was a party or a bar hop going on every weekend. But when the laughter and music stopped, I wondered, *What the hell am I doing?*

I was reasonably happy, but in my youthful innocence I felt dwarfed by how huge the world was, and was desperately trying to figure out my own place in it. The urge to run away had been there for a long time. Maybe that week-long joyride I'd taken with my friends at 17 had been the first symptom of the travelling fever that would eventually grip me.

I couldn't close my eyes to the fantasy. I wanted to get as far away from anyone who had an influence on me, so I'd be free to figure myself out. I'd always been a pleaser, concentrating more on making others happy than on my own *becoming*. I'd lived for a long time under the shadow of my parental figures, very often playing the game according to their rules, and sometimes those rules began to ring so loudly in my head that I couldn't even hear my own voice. I longed for enough silence to do that. I know I'm not alone: almost every young adult has experienced that sensation of being trapped, that need to push out of the narrow confines of childhood and finally be autonomous and accountable to self.

It sounds harsh, but I decided it was my time, and everyone else would have to sit on the back burner for a while. But first, I'd have to finish studying. I'd always had a profound intellectual curiosity, so I'd embraced the opportunity to do an apprenticeship in engineering, fabrication. It meant spending three years in hands-on training, doing classes by night and putting in my work hours by day.

It was hard, maintaining that life balance. With its

fifty-hour work week, the job was draining every ounce of energy I had. I was trying to become the guardian of my baby niece, Faith's daughter, while training for the New Zealand basketball team, and trying to excel at it all. Death began to seem like a reward, like a rest. A dangerous idea indeed.

I kept shoving that whisper from my mind. I was young; I needed to live! I asked myself, when was I most happy? What would I be doing if I could be doing it right now?

Then, as if in divine response, a couple of things happened. I watched a movie called *Into the Wild*, about a young man who, after completing his 'duty' of schooling, searches for ultimate freedom by letting everything go in his world and setting off with nothing but himself. Eventually, he made it to the wilds of Alaska, surviving purely by his wits, endurance and spiritual strength. Although some people thought the main character, Chris McCandless, was selfish for what he did, it sparked an idea in me.

All that spark needed was some kindling.

It came in the form of something as simple as an image in the background catching my eye: I'd left the TV on. There was a picture there, which so entranced me that I couldn't look away. I didn't even know the name of the place shown (and to be honest I still didn't know it until I just Googled it while writing). It was called the Durdle

Door, a natural stone archway in Dorset, England that juts out into the sea. I imagined myself sitting on that cliff face staring out at the arch and the ocean for days, my mind clear. Instead of all this overwhelming life—some of which I had chosen, and some of which I hadn't—I was in a moment, a moment of just being; a time in which I could appreciate what was *around* me instead of what was *happening* to me.

That was it; it was decided. I was going to let go of the death-grip I had on my own life and free-fall into the wild. I wanted to be free, to roam from country to country. I had been to Europe a few times while I was playing tennis, and could never shake its allure. I just wanted to wander, far from home, roaming free.

I set a date, a realistic date: my twenty-eighth birthday—11 February 2017. I would have finished my apprenticeship, and that would mean a substantial raise in pay. The wage of a qualified tradesman. Prior to that, finances had always been tight, especially as I was on my own, flatting with friends, with no financial help from family.

Once I'd passed the student stage, I'd have a year to work and save. Setting that date and vowing to stick to it would prevent me from committing to anything that would get between me and my ultimate freedom, my chance to just *be*.

The journey would be both physical and spiritual. I would be able to discover what people thought about me and what I thought about myself. I would soak up the crushing pressure, grief and confusion I'd been dealing with, while I took a step outside myself.

┃ THE TEST

FOUR YEARS PASSED and I was a few months away from finishing my apprenticeship. I was 26, by then, about to turn 27. Working hard, I finished earlier than I'd thought, even after spending a few months in hospital having surgery to straighten up my bent body. I could finally lie straight in bed, compared to before, when I was almost stuck in a seated position because all my muscles and tendons were shortened from not stretching enough while going through my teens.

They had re-angled and bolted the ends on my femurs, which made my legs straighter, but prevented me from bending my legs much more past 90 degrees. Whereas I used to be able to sit with my legs under me, like the kneeling pose in yoga they call Vajrasana, I no longer could. I had to relearn how to transfer again, as I'd always transferred from a kneeling position. Now I had to have my legs out in front of me. This allowed me to lie straight in bed, and walk with calipers, but my legs became less versatile, and they wouldn't follow my body the same. So although I'm glad for the surgery, I think I lost as much as I gained.

After spending all that time fantasising and making sure the dream survived the brutality of reality ... it was finally going to happen. I didn't need to protect The Thought any longer; it wasn't exciting or scary. It was just the next thing to happen.

We got three weeks off over Christmas when the business where I worked, TUKI Design, closed down (on this side of the world, in New Zealand, it's summer at Christmas). I usually just drove over to the west coast to see Dad for Christmas and then went somewhere for New Year's—all in my car, of course.

Seeing as I'd never backpacked, and had no one to learn from in a wheelchair, I thought that maybe this time I would just backpack around the South Island for a couple of weeks as a test. Gotta be more exciting than just driving, right?

I decided to hitchhike. After all, that would be my major means of transport when I finally embarked on my big trip. Getting around that way over the next couple of weeks would be like chucking myself into the deep end and seeing if I could swim. If I wasn't ready before, I would be now.

It would be a far cry from all the travelling I'd done before, mainly for sport, where my teammates and I could enjoy being spoiled in resorts, having everything pretty much handed to us. I would be surviving by my wits, my charm, the small amount of money I was taking with me, and the kindness of strangers.

I'd got a loan to get the things I thought I'd need. I could have saved up for the NZ$2,000 worth of stuff I ended up buying, but once an idea is in my head, it's stuck on repeat until I either act or write it down. I simply didn't have the patience for the long, slow process of saving my pennies.

I pretty much went shopping and bought everything once. Let's just say I got a bit carried away at the outdoor store. I bought a big, 45-litre hiking backpack, a tent, a sleeping bag, jackets, and other warm clothes.

I also got a pocket knife, travel towel, all-purpose soap (for washing myself or my clothes as needed), a cooker and mini pot, and other bits and pieces I could think of that I'd need for camping and hiking. I must have made my salesperson's day!

High on my list of priorities were Bluetooth wireless headphones. I love music, and I chose Bluetooth because having to struggle with the wires of normal headphones can be a pain in the ass while transferring and trying to control your body in the chair. I can't tell you how many times the cord of a wired device has gotten tangled in my arms, frustrating me and even causing my phone to fall off my lap or chair. It's like trying to do something with those old pig tail cords that home phones used to have—remember those? You always wind up getting tangled in yourself.

Music was, for me, a non-negotiable essential. It enhanced my experience whenever I wanted to soak in the sight of something beautiful. As much as I love the sound of nature, and even the silence, music helps me to stay in my head sometimes, and to enjoy the moment or link a memory to a sound. That way, when I hear the song next time, I remember the moment. It's also great inspiration, and keeps me pumped during long pushes.

My plan was to have no plan. I had a rough idea of where the two weeks would get me. For instance, I knew I was going to Greymouth for Christmas to spend some time with my family. I probably wasn't going to stay more than one night in most places, and I was just going to travel as much as I felt like doing each day.

Normally, driving from the bottom to the top of the south island takes around ten hours, and from east to west around four hours. I planned to just loop around the island. But apart from that, everything was reliant on whether I got rides and how long it took to get them, and whatever detours I fancied taking. But it really was just a go with the flow type of adventure. And this, to me, is the best kind.

THE ADVENTURE: NEW ZEALAND

Taking the first step
23 December 2015

I FINISHED UP AT WORK. It was a half day, which was perfect. I drove home and checked my bags. I knew I'd be hauling around whatever I chose to travel with for the next couple of weeks, but still, I packed a few items that probably turned out to be unnecessary. For example, I got a LifeStraw, which is a filter straw that you can suck water of any quality from any source and it filters it into clean drinking water.

Then there was my travel guitar, an electric guitar that I could plug my headphones into and play to myself, or plug it into an amp or aux cord to entertain others. I'd always been drawn to things where I could express myself—that's why I was drawn to music. Life is so much more beautiful with a dash of music in it. So I

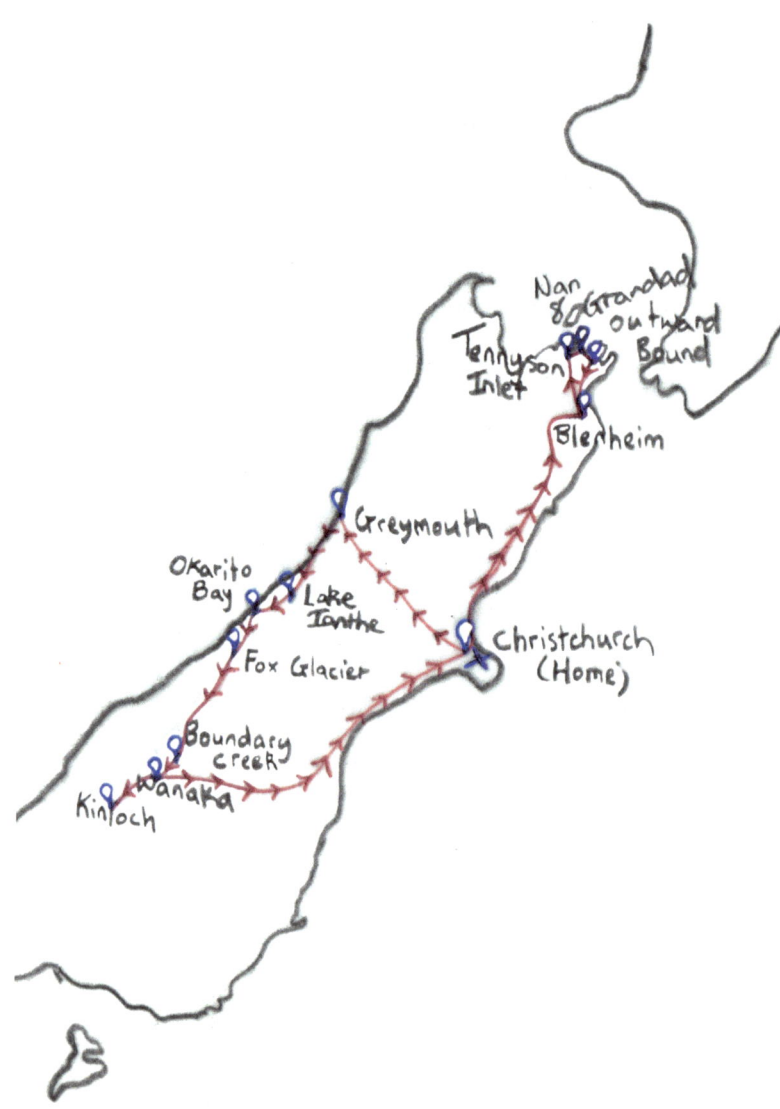

had picked up a guitar and started teaching myself at eighteen, then stopped for a bit until I picked it back up when I was twenty-two. I stuck with teaching myself that time, and have always been more interested in writing my own music rather than playing covers. I liked to use the travel guitar when I met up with friends and played it through the car stereo.

But there were also necessities, items I wouldn't have dreamed of leaving behind, such as a book and my journal, and supplies such as catheters, to avoid having to find a toilet every hour or so.

So my backpack wound up being rather chunky, and I'd have to strap it onto my back for most of my travels. I couldn't put it on the back of my chair as it was too big and heavy; plus, I liked the idea of it being strapped to my body, as that made it seem more normal and also easier to control.

The straps on the backpack make it surprisingly comfortable to wear, even with its size and weight, which forced me to lean forward, otherwise tipping over backwards was inevitable—and it's hard to fall over backwards and look elegant doing it, especially in a wheelchair. This development had come as a surprise to me, as I hadn't practiced pushing or anything with the bag on. Yep; I'd done nothing apart from buy my gear, pack it, and jump into the taxi.

I took a taxi to where the road starts at the edge of Christchurch. It was a perfectly mundane intersection, nothing but pavement, scattered buildings, and a few trees, but I felt a bit like a hobbit about to set foot outside of The Shire for the first time.

Nervousness and excitement were running through my body now. Pushing a little bit up the road from the taxi found me adjusting here and there, figuring out how I was going to balance. When I was sure I was settled … out went the thumb.

It's happening, I told myself, *the sun's shining, the shades are on, and for once I have no idea what was going to happen next. Glorious.*

My first ride showed up within ten minutes. It was a station wagon occupied by three foreign students: a Slovakian, a Columbian and an Indian. Two men and one woman, all around my age. They were off to tramp in Fox Glacier, on the South Island's west coast.

My pack was heavier than I'd thought. The Slovakian guy gave me a hand to take it off because, embarrassingly, I was struggling and almost flipped over backwards, just as I'd predicted. I tried not to let it bother me too much, reminding myself that I'd eventually get it sussed.

Christchurch to Greymouth is a three-and-a-half-hour drive, through the Canterbury Plains and then through the southern alps, emerging on the other side on the west coast. As we drove, the country opened up before me, stretching out, green and full of promise. I'd moved around so much as a child—more than I'd wanted to—and had driven this same road many times. I'd passed through here by bus when I was younger, so the sights, though impressive, weren't new to me. But today, everything seemed fresh to my eyes, and full of promise.

Life can harden you to any situation, making the strangest predicament seem normal. I was nervous, as I'd never taken a ride from a stranger, although as a kid I remember hitchhiking with Mum once. It was my first time hitching alone, and the first time I hadn't had something pre-planned like a bus or ride organised. I was probably noticeably excited. I made small talk with these three kind strangers who'd picked me up, still not sure how to relax in these circumstances.

They dropped me off at Kumara Junction, and I left my name and number with them in case they ever needed someone local to help them. The junction is dull, flat and unremarkable, and marks the halfway point between Hokitika to the south and Greymouth to the north.

I wasn't far from a town that had some significance for me: Kumara, where the population stood at around 300 people, 20 minutes from that bare patch of land where my family and I once had our house bus. That was the place where, at the age of ten, I'd first had that half-shaped inspiration to spread my wings. So I suppose there was a bit of a Karmic echo there. (By the way, 'kumara' is also what we call a sweet potato in New Zealand!)

My second ride was from a young guy from Greymouth, who'd just finished a shift at a meatworks nearby and was heading home. He was chatty and easy to get along with and dropped me at the train station in Greymouth. It's the largest town on the west coast, with a population of around 14,000 people, and, like Kumara, it held memories for me, although not necessarily brilliant ones.

I went to high school there for half a year and then, between the ages of 11 and 13, to intermediate school. I would describe Greymouth as a town that's still in the past. I remember it like this: the movies at the theatre were always half a year behind and shops were closed on a Sunday. For a young person there really isn't much to do here. When I think of *Greymouth* I think of grey skies with a grey personality; no colour at all, despite its beautiful native bush. It's the kind of place people with inspiration try and leave. It's bordered by a rugged beach on one side, and on the other, the Grey River meets the sea. It's protected by big flood banks, in response to "the great flood" of 1988.

Since our family hardly ever sees each other—Dad and I speak maybe four to six times a year—we all make an effort on Christmas to pay him a visit. Since I moved out at 14, Christmas became the one yearly visit I was sure to make. Before I had a car, I simply caught a tour bus over.

Malachy tends to move between the west coast and Christchurch. He's a roamer, like me, never staying in any one place very long, so it's hard to remember where he is. He could have been staying at a friend's one night and then at Dad's the next—and then with another family friend the week. The two of us probably see each other the most, as we sometimes work in the same city, and try to hold on to our brotherly bond. But still, it could have been a couple of months since I'd seen him. When I called, he was already at Dad's house.

It was late afternoon, around 5.00 p.m., and still light out as it doesn't get dark until around 10.00 in the summer in New Zealand. I'd been hitchhiking for half a day when he came to pick me up.

I hadn't warned them I was coming, but the revelation that I was on an adventure was no big deal. West coast people are free spirits; a career in a bustling city is definitely not at the top of many priority lists, and my family already had a history of moving around, from home to home and job to job. So hitchhiking across New Zealand didn't sound too unusual. They certainly weren't worried about me. The overall vibe amounted to, *Cool, have an awesome trip, and give me a message to let me know you're safe at some stage!*

Christmas Day, 2015

WE SPENT A COUPLE OF NIGHTS at Dad's for Christmas. It's nice to go visit, because there's no pressure and everything's very relaxed, but it's certainly not a challenging or exciting environment. Traditionally, we go around to friends' houses and chow down on Christmas goodies. It was enjoyable, and important to me because sometimes I get caught up in my own life and never see anyone. It's nice to keep in touch with people.

Christmas in New Zealand has a different feel about it than the images you see in movies and TV shows coming out of countries like the US and the UK. Remember, it's summer in the southern hemisphere, and most people get a break, so a lot of the time people go camping with families and friends, have outdoor BBQs and indulge in a Christmas beer—or several. For a non-Kiwi it might seem more like a summer vacation vibe.

Looking around at my family laughing and sharing a holiday meal, and at the kids opening their presents and playing, I thought of how much—and how fast—I'd grown up. When I was a child, it was about presents. It's the same as every other family, I imagine; waking up early and begging our parents to let us open up presents and eat a tonne of dessert. (They were even sneaky enough to hold Christmas against us, threatening to cancel it if we were naughty!) The only minor difference was that in my family, Christmas celebrations were never held at the same place. There was never the same routine, especially since the season usually met us living in a different house. When I left home as a teen, it became less about presents and more about making sure I had a family, and not to get so caught up in moving forward that I never saw them.

Not having Mum there that time felt normal, to be honest, but I felt Faith's absence. Christmas was about family, and one member of my family would forever be missing.

Boxing Day, 2015

I WOKE UP ON BOXING DAY a bit hungover—okay, maybe *very* hungover. It was the first real part of the journey, and I was excited to get on the road, and into the unknown.

Dad saw me off with his usual sarcastic warning: "Don't do anything I wouldn't do—and if you do, don't get caught," but that's something I've been hearing my whole life, so I took it as a sign of encouragement.

I made my way to Hokitika. It's a beach-side just south-west of Greymouth, with a decent view of the alps. I wanted to visit my little sisters, Shadow and

Keira. They live with their mother, since she and my father didn't stay together after their birth. It was good to see them, and I think it's especially important that they have a connection with their big brother and the rest of their family.

A few hours later, heaving the big backpack back onto my back (doing slightly better than I did on my first ride), I waved them goodbye from the main road on that beautiful summer's day.

There's a bridge that crosses the Hokitika River. A separate footpath running alongside the road makes it safe to cross on foot, bike, or wheelchair, and it's worth stopping halfway across to appreciate the beautiful views from all angles. I'm not particularly afraid of heights—well, no more afraid than any normal person—but crossing made my heart thump. It was a symbolic moment; I felt as if I was crossing a threshold from the tedium and uncertainty of my old life and into something mysterious and new.

As I crossed, I ran into a guy on a bike who was coming towards me, heading back into town. I assumed he'd been down at the river on the other side. We stopped and chatted for maybe five or ten minutes. He told me his name was Graham, and that he made jade stone jewellery from home. He was a cool dude, and I took the encounter as an omen that I'd be meeting many new and interesting characters over the next couple of weeks. As it turned out, I was right.

I pushed across the rest of the bridge; it was such a beautiful day on the coast. I could see the ocean and, looking down, a road winding into the native bush.

As I sat on the other side with my thumb out, waiting, a guy I knew from Christchurch stopped in his van. He's also in a chair himself. What were the chances? He was with his wife and son. They were heading not too far up the road to camp, and the van was crammed with outdoor gear, including a kayak. We did pass a few moments having a friendly yarn, though—that's a casual chat, for all you non-Kiwis. They offered me a ride, but I was too eager to keep going, and the place I wanted to spend my first night alone was an hour or so away. I passed on the ride, we said our goodbyes, and I waited.

Across the Hokitika Bridge, taken from a friend in a van.

I sat there with my headphones on, listening to one of the playlists I'm always mixing, a blend of old and new music. Depending on my energy levels, my go-to might range from classical to electronic. If I'm feeling nostalgic for my childhood, I listen to some 90s rock. Over the rest of my adventures, I would find myself turning to music again and again, downloading hour-long playlists with "chill mix" or "summer mix" in the title and see where it took me.

In just ten short minutes, a man from Uruguay picked me up. He didn't speak great English, but it was a lot better than the ten or so words that I knew in Spanish. During my travels with sport, language was never much of a barrier, and it wasn't now. I usually ended up just learning just a few essential words, like 'hello' and 'thank you', and some odd words I discovered by accident, like 'fork' or 'battery', that ended up sticking in my head. Funny enough, I avoided saying the word 'tent' any time I spoke to someone who wasn't from New Zealand. I kept getting funny looks and confusion, because our 'tent' sounds like 'tint', as our vowels for the 'e' and 'i' switch around in the Kiwi accent. To make things even more confusing, our 'i's sound like 'u's, so sounds like 'fish and chips' come out like 'fush and chups'. Even now I avoid it, put on an American accent for it, or just say 'camping gear'. Ah, language!

We managed to communicate, and an hour later the driver dropped me off at my first stop, Lake Ianthe, a beautiful expanse of deep blue on the west coast. It was a fairly popular camping spot; people would stop there and sleep in their van or camper or to go out on a small boat for the day fishing. There were no toilets; it was just a question of recycling back into nature—if you want to put a positive spin on it.

There was a small grassy patch right next to the lake that looked ideal to me; the view was beautiful, and if I'd been alone it would have been blissful, but it looked like other people here had had the same idea.

There wasn't much to explore at Ianthe; the campsite was a little area off the side of the road. Although I wasn't all that far away from where I'd begun the day, I'd spent so much time dilly-dallying with my sisters, and chatting with the friends and strangers I'd met along the way that by then the day was waning. It was time to get ready to face the night.

Before leaving home, I'd had one practice at putting up the tent in the backyard so I wouldn't look too silly struggling like a city man putting it up in front of other people. Though I'd set my tent up without too much struggling, it still would have been nice to have been away from other campers. I wouldn't have minded a swim, but I was nervous with the people around. I didn't necessarily need any witnesses as I began to push my boundaries by going down into the water.

I had a quick meal, the usual camping cliché of quickly heated beans. The lack of luxury didn't bother me. I've always seen food as a fuel for my sport, and also, I lost my sense of smell when I was 16, after I accidentally whacked myself in the nose with my tennis racquet. They say your sense of smell greatly impacts on your sense of taste, and I pretty much eat anything that doesn't have a strange texture, so I guess this is true. I tell people I can just taste salty, sweet, bitter and sour. It's helpful with my nutrition plans for sport and makes them easy to stick to. So … beans for dinner? No problem.

I decided I'd make more of an effort the next day to find somewhere just as beautiful, but where I'd be on my own. Getting away earlier than I thought would also mean that I'd have more time to travel. The next day would be my first full day. I planned to get up early, breathe in the dawn air, and then pack up. Dad had given me an old film camera, which I wasn't sure I knew how to use yet, and I was looking forward to how terrible the photos would come out after developing them.

Even sleeping on the ground in a strange place didn't faze me. I've always had a knack for sleeping anywhere at any time. I once made a bet with a friend that I could go to sleep on my knees at a party … and won. My sleeping bag was the most expensive item I'd bought, and with good reason. It was very comfortable to sleep in, and for that I was grateful. I did wake up a few times with dead arms though, as the ground was hard, even though I'd picked the area with the softest grass. If you ever saw a paraplegic wake up with dead arms, I am sure you'd laugh. I kind of roll and wiggle, trying to sit up until my arms start to get some blood flow.

Still suffering the effects of all that Christmas food and alcohol, I fell asleep soon after writing in my diary. Sunset was around ten, but I fell asleep in the dark, so it was pretty late.

27 December 2015

I WAS PLANNING TO GET UP at 5.50 a.m. to watch the sunrise. I've seen a lot of sunsets—if you know what I mean—but not many rises. You guessed it; I slept in to 8.30, so I well and truly missed it.

I had my first coffee, tent style, boiling it up in the pot and cooker I'd brought. There were to be no gourmet "glamping"-type meals on this trip. Cooking was never a big thing in my family and I never got any joy out of it. The more time I was in the kitchen the less time I had to do the things I wanted to. So I generally eat healthy but very simply. All I needed was a full stomach and adequate hydration. And, of course, coffee to keep my turbo boosted.

It was quite scary trying to not look too disabled carrying my pack in front of my temporary neighbours, though I think I pulled it off. I even pushed up a gravel road with the pack on. With no one around, these things are easy because it takes as long as it takes, and I know I can figure out a way to do it. But when there are onlookers … or when my mind tricks me into thinking there are … it's a different story.

It was another stunning day. Murray from Geraldine picked me up in his 4WD truck and took me to his "bach"—his holiday home—in Okarito, a beautiful beach village just past Hari Hari. He was in his late 40s or early 50s, grey-haired and stocky and dressed in a typical west coast getup; gumboots, t-shirt and shorts.

We got there about eleven in the morning, and Murray gave me until about two to have a look around, which was plenty of time as Okarito is tiny. I whipped off my shirt and started up the Okarito wetland walk, pushing up a steep gravel track. Thank God I'd left my pack in his truck! It didn't bother me that I'd left all my worldly goods in a stranger's car. I think I have a pretty good instinct about who's trustworthy. Even so, I tend to trust most people until the trust is lost instead of the other way around, of not trusting in the first instance. That might not always be street smart, but it feels good. Besides, that was all part and parcel of the hitchhiking life.

The coolest thing about that stop was making two new friends: Deb and Ian. They were an older couple, and I got the impression they'd lived there for a while. I was fine with being approached by strangers; it was doing the approaching myself that always got me nervous or self-conscious. In fact, I like talking to strangers, it's nice to have a conversation with someone who doesn't know anything about you, and I know nothing about them.

After I'd finished the track, Deb came up to me and invited me in for some chicken soup, which, of course, I wasn't going to turn down, seeing as I'd only had rolled oats and baked beans. (I made a note to do a better shop next time I was at the supermarket.)

Deb was lovely, and so was Ian. They were the type of people willing to let strangers into their house and look after them. Also, Deb had taken in a girl the same age as me. Deb mentioned an accident, but only in passing. The girl seemed sweet, too; a bit shy, cute and soft-spoken. I got the feeling she was recovering from something, that she was broken but now on the path to recovery. I filled up on soup, chatted awhile, thanked them, and then pushed my way back down the beach until Murray was done.

Fox Glacier

I JUMPED BACK IN with Murray around two o'clock and together we headed down to Fox Glacier, hoping to see somewhere on the side of the road to camp the night, but no such luck. He was continuing on way farther than I wanted to go in one day, heading to his home somewhere with a name I didn't recognise. It was time to part ways. He pulled to the side and let me out. I pulled into a café, got a coffee, and then rang a caravan park. They had one spot left, so that sucked up twenty bucks.

Another traveller, Sarah, and I were the only ones tenting, so I said gidday. We bonded immediately. She took me up to Lake Matheson and we walked around the lake, chatting away. It turned out she was fifty-one; I couldn't believe it. Sarah had a surfer-type look and personality, and at first glance, I took her for about 30.

The view was breathtaking. The waters of the lake reflected the brilliant blue of the sky, and the mountains in the distance loomed. We made it halfway around the lake before we got blocked by some stairs. I didn't feel the need to climb them; people are already stunned enough at the idea of seeing a person in a chair hitchhiking, but to be pushing along these tracks … it's quite a test.

It was lovely talking to Sarah. Nice to have someone send me into that depth of thought, past the mundanities of working and paying rent. I always appreciate another point of view. Her tent was just a few metres away from mine. We settled in for the evening.

I had to leave the wheelchair outside my tent. I tied one of the tent's guy ropes to it just in case someone who'd had a few too many beers decided to take it for a joyride. There was a drizzle, so it got a bit wet overnight.

I could have probably stayed another night there at Fox Glacier, because they have showers and it was easy, but the call of adventure was loud in my ears. I needed to keep going. The next stop on my list was Haast.

| *Lake Wanaka*
28 December 2015

A 7.30 AM RISE AND SHINE and no sign of Sarah. I had heard her rustling around in the morning, so I'd assumed she'd gone on the walk she'd wanted to. I'd been hoping to see her around.

Bloody tent condensation was dripping on the sleeping bag and, though I'm no expert by any means, I'm sure you shouldn't don't get down wet. There had to be a strategy for stopping that from happening. I also had to pick where to set up the tent better next time, because both mornings I had had to wait till the sun got to the tent to dry it out, and trying to fumble the tent and push the chair across campgrounds could end in disaster.

It was my second day of eating beans, and I was already keen for something different—not that I was complaining, because I was just happy to have food.

I had a pressure sore on my arse, which is a pain if you're sitting in the chair all the time. I think it was from all the basketball and handcycling that I'd been doing before I left home. It doesn't help when you don't have much of an arse to start with. So I was on a mission to try to manage that, because a lot of the time, my legs go into spasm because of the sores, and legs are hard to control at the best of times. But I had plasters, so it wasn't all bad.

Right; let's sort this tent out.

I got the tent dry and left Sarah a note, then got out on the road at about 10.30 A.M. I was full of anticipation, and the long, undulating road stretched out before me into the wide green yonder.

A young guy, Dylan, picked me up from Fox Glacier. He was a twenty-three-year-old mechanic from Queenstown who was up in Hoki (Hokitika) visiting family. We stopped in Haast, which was where I was originally going. It's a small beachside town sandwiched between two mountains, with a lot of satisfying wilderness to explore. After this, the scenery would change, as I would begin moving inland, away from the coast.

There was an i-SITE visitor information centre, there, so I checked it out to see if there were any campsites on the way to Wanaka, and also to get coffee and some lunch. Dylan had it way more together than I did when I was twenty-three, and I'm always proud of young people when they figure it out and have that drive for life. We listened to some cool music on the way and it was a relaxed drive down to the next stop. Boundary Creek was the stop of choice. There was an accessible campsite near Lake Wanaka, quite windy, but so beautiful.

The wind was certainly going to be a good test of the tent—I half wished I'd taken the extra pegs I'd given to Sarah to help keep her tent to the ground ... darn!

Soon, the tent was up. It was another scorcher of a day; I had to semi stay hydrated and the water there was a bit dodgy, or so the sign said. I got to try out my LifeStraw, which filters it clean. In case you're curious, there's not much difference in taste, but it takes quite a bit of effort to suck the water all the way through those fine filters. It's a lifesaver for many, I'm sure, who don't have easy access to safe drinking water, but for now I decided I'd stick to the bottled kind.

It was so lovely being in an area where my phone was useless, to be on my own and have this beautiful view of a lake and mountains. I was excited to know that the next day I'd be meeting up with some friends, Josh and Ayla. Josh and I went to the same high school; we'd never spoked a word to each other then, but as the years went on and the parties started dying down, we started to become closer … also, I dated Ayla's sister, Saffron, who was my first proper girlfriend, and that was how they'd met. I guess that helped too …. I was even best man at their wedding. Would not have expected that when we were 15!

The only way I was going to know if we were still meeting in Queenstown was when I could send a text, if I came into an area where there was phone signal. In the meantime, I was enjoying all this nature and beauty, and most of all meeting new people. They were restoring my faith in humanity. I'd been expecting it to be a lot harder to get rides, that people would be reluctant to pick up a stranger in a wheelchair. I wasn't sure it would be easy to slip into conversation with them, either. But stepping out into the world like this broadened my appreciation for the wide variety of people there are out there.

So far, my New Zealand lark had been a tester for the big journey, and I still felt like there was a time limit on it. I wondered how it would feel when I could spend as much time as I wanted at a place when there might not be anyone else around? In terms of my gear, it all seemed to be sweet and I hadn't had that thought like, 'Shit, I need that' or, 'I wish I'd brought that'. The last two days had been beautiful, but I was still on a time schedule and I didn't like that.

Going The Wrong Way
29 December 2015

I WOKE UP TO DISCOVER I was being wasted by sandflies, dense clouds of black dots that latched onto your skin and sucked your blood. They're maybe not was dangerous as mosquitos in terms of disease transmission, but they sure are as irritating. I packed up my tent and got on my way as quickly as possible. I pushed up the hill out of Boundary Creek—and let me tell you, that was a *mission*. I think I had the pack straps adjusted wrong because I was struggling. To get power into a push in a wheelchair, you have to lean forward and put your weight into it—especially if that push is up a hill, and unfortunately every time I leant forward, the bottom of the bag would get caught on my backrest. So think yourself lucky when next you're walking up a hill with your backpack!

I thought coming out of the spot and hitching a ride was going to be a difficult that day, as it was a winding road and drivers didn't have much time to see me and slow down. I made a sign saying QUEENSTOWN—not sure why, because there was only one road there.

As I waited, an older fellow on a bike stopped and I had a quick yarn to him. I missed a few ride opportunities, but a good yarn is worth it. Besides, meeting others was part of my mission.

A young Swiss couple picked me up. They'd been staying at Boundary Creek that night too, and to be honest, if someone leaving the campsite didn't pick me up, I could have been waiting awhile. Back at the campsite, they'd looked like they were in love, which was cute to see.

They took me to Wanaka, and on the way I rang Josh to see if they were in Queenstown. They told me to meet in Arrowtown, so I started wheeling towards the entrance to Wanaka, which I thought was the right direction to start hitchhiking. At that end of Wanaka, a hill rises, leading to the spot where I needed to be to stick my thumb out. This was the first time I had had to ask for help with my backpack. I think I asked because Wanaka was thronging and there was an endless flow of cars, full of people I knew would have seen me try. I could've done it on my own, but it would have been painful to watch. It's not painful to do and it doesn't bother me if no one is watching, but I knew someone would offer to help if I didn't ask, and that would have been embarrassing. Super nice of them, but embarrassing.

So I asked a couple to carry my bag to the top of the hill for me. I then stuck my sign out and waited. Someone pulled over and told me they were going to Christchurch. I asked if they could drop me off at Arrowtown on the way … turns out I was at the wrong end of Wanaka. He showed me my location on Google maps. I thanked him for stopping and telling me. As it turned out, the sign hadn't helped me get a ride, but it had helped me not go in the wrong direction.

Before going up the (wrong) hill, I'd told Josh I was leaving Wanaka, so I felt like I was running a bit late. I boosted through town and asked a passer-by if I was heading in the right direction—I didn't want to make the same mistake twice. I'd literally just wheeled past the road that lead to Arrowtown!

Lucky I'd asked.

| *Arrowtown and Kinloch*

I MET A FRIENDLY LADY on her daily stroll who had a cousin in the States, so I had a bit of a yarn with her. I had to tell her I should be on my way as I might

Josh and Ayla take in the serenity of Lake Wanaka.

miss Josh and Ayla. I was reluctant to cut our chat short, because as long as someone is willing to talk to me, I'm willing to talk to them.

I stuck my thumb out in the right direction this time, and a couple of seventeen-year-olds picked me up. They were cool and offered me a beer, so I couldn't decline that … plus, it was so hot. As it turned out, I was lucky to have good weather throughout my entire trip, since the weather in New Zealand can be temperamental, and changes according to the whim of the gods. The west coast of the south island is all native bush, green due to the rainfall, and as the weather comes over the alps it dries out. I was brown after a few days hitching and was putting sunscreen on three to four times a day.

Having a beer with them reminded me of when I was seventeen: knew it all but actually knew nothing. Knew how to have fun, that's for sure. I gave one of them my number so that if I went to Queenstown, I could try and get one of them into the pub with me, as the drinking age in New Zealand is eighteen. Nothing wrong with having a little fun by bending the rules, I feel, especially when you're young.

They dropped me off at the turn-off to Arrowtown, supplied me with a beer for the road and left me on my merry way. Arrowtown is a small historical town between Queenstown and Wanaka. It's so quaint I couldn't help but feel like there should be a horse and cart trundling down the middle of the street.

I stressed out a bit that I had lost my sunglasses (they weren't cheap), but they were just in the truck. I whipped my shirt off, embraced the sun, and waited for Josh to come get me.

I had lunch and chilled out in Arrowtown for a while with Josh and Ayla while trying to adjust to being around someone I knew again, and to the fact that I didn't have to put myself out there and having it feel pretty comfortable. Weird feeling. They were having the same issue after being on their own for a week. It had only been three days for me! But, wow, had it been cool and exciting having to put myself outside my comfort zone.

We left Arrowtown and tried to find somewhere to stay. After driving a while around Lake Wakatipu, we found a hidden paradise: Kinloch, a beautiful Department of Conservation campground in the middle of nowhere right on the lake, with the cutest café, which seemed so odd to be in the nowhere place. There's an odd little road around the lake, which left you with the feeling that maybe you took the wrong turn.

Most of these sites I ended up staying at were D.O.C. campsites like that one. They're run by the government, and for many you pay by dropping your fee into an honesty box. The fee depended on the facilities. Basic campsites (which are just a spot that you're allowed to camp in, and which can be found anywhere in NZ and are often super beautiful) are free. Better equipped sites, those with amenities like toilets, cost between $7.50 and $15 NZ dollars a head, while the serviced campsites charged $20. These are all located at weird and wonderful places.

I jumped into the lake off a wharf—partly to clean my clothes, partly to cool down. After our swim, we had dinner together, then had a sing-song with the guitars we'd brought. I sat on the beach, feeling the wind in my face and looking over the lake after the sun had just set, writing in my journal: beautiful.

I'd been pushing myself a lot this trip with what I did with the wheelchair and especially who saw me do it. It has always been hard to blend in; a wheelchair can't be as well hidden as a blemish or rip in your jeans. Even on my most confident days I was conscious of who was around and what I did—and whether it would make me look like I needed help.

I had put myself in a position where there was no choice but to keep moving whether I was self-conscious or not.

I'll never get tired of listening to the waves ….

30 December 2015

DAY TWO OF NOT BEING ON MY OWN, and it was more effort than being a solo traveller. Having to make decisions together and be aware of another perspective takes away just a bit from your sense of autonomy. I think that goes without saying, though.

We packed up and headed into Wanaka to meet up with another couple of friends, Ashlea and Sam. We'd all decided to camp together there, as that particular campsite was walking distance from the town centre and also a lot cheaper than staying in a hotel—plus there is something about camping with a bunch of friends.

For the romantics among you, let me share a little

side note about Ashlea: I'd actually asked her to be my girlfriend when I was ten years old. I even gave her mum flowers before we moved from Owaka.

Even the way we reconnected was funny. When I was about 20, I remember waking up after a big night in the Christchurch nightclubs and discovering a random number in my phone. So naturally, I texted it—who knew where that would lead, right? Turned out it was Ashlea. She recognized this guy in the wheelchair at the nightclub. This happens a lot; people recognize me but I don't them, I am guessing because I get stuck in the memory easier with the chair.

I couldn't remember trying to romance her when we were kids, as I'm sure I did a lot of strange things when I was that age, but it was romantic meeting back up again ten years later. So we dated for the briefest time, purely out of nostalgia, but ended up good friends instead. To this day, Ashlea is tight in my circle of friends.

As we all set up our tents, I realised how busy it was. Wanaka is an adventure tourism hub in the South Island, surrounded by a beautiful lake and picturesque mountains. Like Queenstown, Wanaka represents the image most people have of New Zealand: 100% pure. Whatever picture that you have in your mind of New Zealand, you'll probably find it here. Adventure tourism is one of New Zealand's biggest sources of income, and

Wanaka is a part of that: you can jet boat, kayak, hike, mountain bike—pretty much anything extreme and outdoorsy. It was draining trying to fit into this tourist town, and I was very much looking forward to being back out on my own in the uncertainty again.

Rolling into a New Year
New Year's Day 2016

I WOKE UP SO HUNGRY from the night before. I'd had a few too many drinks celebrating New Year's. The last couple of days I'd been staying at the Wanaka Top 10 Holiday Park. We'd all been cruising around checking out the touristy-ness of it all. I'd also been to a barber and had my beard shaved off—why, I can't say. Maybe it was in keeping with my newfound go-with-the-flow attitude. Sometimes I just decide I need a different interaction with people, or need to present myself in a different way. Change is my friend, something I'm used to, I think. So, anyway, it was a brand-new year and I was back to no chin again!

The night before, we'd had a BBQ and a few drinks to ring in 2016, and then headed down to the waterfront to see the band and watch the fireworks. The band was memorable for being unmemorable. Although the celebrations took place outdoors on a big stage sitting in front of the water, there was no dance floor. People were just standing around, waiting for the fireworks.

As I've mentioned (probably more than once), drinking has been the biggest struggle in my life, and I've always managed to cross the line with it. I remember being on a different level of buzz than my friends; they were very chill, but the alcohol had made me more eager to ramp up my energy. This was a common occurrence for me, and my friends knew it. The drinks followed one after another, and then I made my way into the town by myself to roll around, talking to people and listening to music in the nightclub.

I eventually left my friends just after midnight. If I'd stayed any longer, I knew I'd be bringing trouble back on myself. I was addicted to the euphoria drinking brought me, the false courage, the death of my shyness. When I drank too much, I became the centre of attention, and I loved it. So it was time to go home.

When I woke up, I packed up the tent in the scorching heat. Everyone else had left, but I had to do a load of washing and sort my life out, shoving past a raging hangover. I thought I was dying—part of me had to admit I deserved it, since I'd brought it on myself. To make it harder, at some point during the night I'd broken a tent pole; I don't even want to ask myself how. I spent a while trying to dis-assemble it. Instant karma.

While waiting for the washing to finish, I met a cool chick from Switzerland who was travelling around. We chatted awhile, and then I also had a yarn with the longer-term residents of the campground who talked about the young people who drifted in and out of the campsite, and all the adventures they shared.

Eventually, I was all packed; I wheeled on down through Wanaka to the spot I was at the other day when I'd managed to get lost. This time I was able to determine I was in the right place, despite my splitting headache and the fact that my body wasn't feeling quite up to pushing up the Wanaka hill with the pack on my back, but it was good to sweat out the stale booze. A fitting punishment. I hoped it would teach me a lesson for next time I considered guzzling down another bottle of the devil's swill.

I was hoping to catch a ride straight to Christchurch. Although in a way it was like taking a step backward, it just made sense. I'd decided to start that loop back up to the top of the south island. Christchurch was on the way up, and the hitchhiking would be good because most people leaving from Wanaka going this direction were headed there, as it's the biggest city in the south island.

Because of my escapades the night before, I ended up starting the day too late, anyway, and it would have been dark soon. The idea of getting home to my bed and having a shower, using my own toilet, was way too appealing; a free and luxurious pitstop along the way.

I settled on a good hitchhiker's spot and had a couple of offers to drop me further up, but I had a tree with shade which seemed perfect, so I stayed put. A guy pulled over in a 4WD and told me it would be easier to hitch from the corner further up, so I jumped in and abandoned the comfy shadow of the tree.

No shade on this corner. I took off the pack, removed my shirt, and tried to relax in the heat, the sun beaming down on me. After fifteen minutes or so of waiting, an older couple from New South Wales, Australia, picked me up. They were going to Alexandra, which wasn't really where I wanted to go, which I found out while looking at a map printed on the back of a DOC campsite brochure I'd brought with me. But I was thankful to be in the air-conditioned car in the state I was in.

I accepted the fact that I'd either have to pay for somewhere to stay in Alexandra or put the tent up—which wasn't what I quite felt like doing that day. It was 5.00 P.M. by then, thanks to me getting up late and taking most of the day to organise myself, and I knew it would be harder to sort everything out.

We got to Cromwell, which is about five hours out of Christchurch, and I made a quick decision to drop out there after looking at the map. I'd either try get back to Christchurch from there or set up for the night. Cromwell was the last turn-off to go back up to Christchurch and then make my way to the Marlborough Sounds.

Again pushing out in the heat, I stopped often to drink water, which was my best friend that day. I pushed a couple of kilometres along the side of the road and over the Cromwell bridge to the turn-off, stuck out the old thumb and waited with the music on. This spot was the hottest, with no shade, so I had to keep putting the jacket on to half protect me from the sun. I tan quite easily, thanks to the Maori blood I got from Mum, so I wasn't afraid of burning to a crisp. I've never given skin cancer much of thought, either. But the heat was uncomfortable enough to warrant evasive measures.

While I was waiting, I had a chat with a lady who was watching her husband and son swim down at the lake. An hour passed and I was starting to think I might be having to wait in the dark, because I was determined not to set the tent up that night. I think most people were in convoys heading home, so they were on a mission and didn't want to pick up a hitchhiker. Then two cars stopped at the same time, but I could only see one, so when a younger chick who was also hitchhiking boosted off, I thought, *Bugger, back to waiting*. But once she pulled away, I saw another car there. What are the chances of having two cars stop at the same time?

I forget the name of the girl who picked me up—my brain wasn't functioning as it should have been—but she was 28 and from the Czech Republic, and had spent New Year's down at a lake by Wanaka for the last five days and was heading back up to Christchurch … Hallelujah! I could relax and make it home to bed for the night. I got back to Christchurch at about 11.00 p.m. and crashed out instantly—Zzzzzzzz.

Back to Christchurch … But Not for Long

2 January 2016

I WOKE UP AT NINE, and it was pretty bloody nice to wake up at home. I got some groceries and bought a charger cord, as I'd somehow lost mine on the way. I rang Josh, who'd returned to Christchurch, and another best friend of mine, Stephen, to see if they wanted to get a coffee before I headed back out on the road. Stephen was on my side of town, which was perfect, so I just waited around home until noon, when I could catch a ride with him to the drop-off point and of course have a coffee.

I planned on hitching to Blenheim, and the motorway to Blenheim is on the other side of Christchurch. It worked out perfectly. I rang my aunty in Blenheim to see if I could stay the night if I made it up there in time; otherwise I had a DOC campsite in mind. I also rang another friend, Tim, who was up in Marlborough Sounds and said I'd be there within a couple of days. I was all set for the next step of my wanderings.

Friends have been the most beautiful and consistent thing in my life, as I am sure most people can relate. I'm the type of person who takes too many risks and can be a bit *too* free sometimes with my life choices and without these rocks in my life I would have struggled, been broken. I make time for my friends—and all people really—because as much as I love my own company, I know what people have done for me and some things are just more beautiful when shared.

After a couple hours of coffee and conversation, Stephen dropped me off at the outer edge of the city, where the suburbs meet the open road. I had to put a jacket on and pull the rain hood over the bag, as it was drizzling a little bit—enough to get everything wet if I ended up waiting a while. It was the first sign of rain this whole trip, a nice change from the sun, which the body had seen a lot of recently. I'd even made a sign saying 'Blenheim' in the hopes of getting a ride straight there.

I was in luck. After a twenty-minute wait, Robin pulled over but parked a wee way up the road, so I didn't see him. I thought he was just a person going for a run in the rain who wanted to chat (haha) until he asked where I was going. He was going to Blenheim, so that was a bonus.

Blenheim is a small sunny town near the top of the south island, with a population of just about 31,000. It is mainly known for its wineries, so travellers come in to do the seasonal work. It's there in my memories as a flat, sunny and green town surrounded by rolling hills. A pleasurable pitstop on my journey.

Robin was an interesting guy; a doctor from Britain who'd just come from Mount Cook after doing some mountaineering. He made for some interesting conversation on the way up, although I think my brain was still a bit foggy from New Year's: yes, I'd indulged that much. We covered a lot of topics: life, his travels when he was younger (he actually gave me some pointers for my next overseas trip), psychology—everything, really.

After what seemed like a short trip (probably because we were gabbing the whole way), Robin dropped me off at the i-Site in Blenheim, and Aunty Hillary's partner, Ken, came and picked me up. Once I got to her place, we caught up for a bit and met the kitten they had rescued, and then went for a wine at the pub and then a Thai restaurant for dinner.

I thought about heading over later to a pub I'd spotted across the road from the Thai restaurant, without them, and sipping away at some water, listening to some music and meeting some more people, but figured it might be a bit rude, and plus, I wouldn't mind getting up early to spend some time with them before I made way to the Marlborough Sounds the next day. I rolled into bed at 10.41, which for me was a pretty early night.

3 January 2016

ANOTHER CRUISY DAY; it's great when family has your back and you don't have to wake up in a damp tent and wrangle with tent pegs! Instead, I woke up to the luxury of a house and a bed, and had a shower.

After breakfast and a few games of Scrabble with Aunty Hillary and Ken, I went out for a push up a short walking track with Hillary, Ken and Walter, a family friend of Hillary's. I didn't really know him. He was a big man with a big presence. It was quite nice wheeling in the rain.

Hillary dropped me off in Rai Valley, which is 70K away, about halfway between Nelson and Blenheim. I'd rung Tim and he was in Nelson, in Pelorus Sound, about an hour's drive away, so it worked out perfectly that I could get dropped there, and then Tim could pick me up and take me to his "bach"—his house by the beach.

Tim's mum's partner owned it, and in the holidays Tim would take his boat up here and spend a weekend fishing and enjoying the scenery.

It seemed like the day was a little too easy, actually; it didn't exactly fill into the tough guy roughing it narrative! We got to the beautiful part of Tennyson Inlet, where the bach is, surrounded by bushy mountains and beautiful water. I went for a wee push and tried to take another selfie with the camera, which I was sure would be amusing when I developed it —selfies old-school style are not easy! (Spoiler alert; it was hilarious.)

We settled for dinner and DVDs that night, as the weather was terrible. Hopefully, the next day we'd be able to get out on the kayaks do some fishing.

| Outward Bound, Anakiwa
4 January 2016

BUT, NAH. It was too rough out in the bay for the kayaks. Instead, I went for a walk with Tim, his partner and mum, who were on a New Year's break, and the dogs. I decided to ask Tim if he could drop me in Rai Valley so I could go to a place with cell phone reception to sort out going to Nana's. Getting to Nana's meant ringing her for the number of the mailman, who, I was told, I could catch a ride with to Raetihi Bay in the Kenepuru Sounds. My grandparents lived a two-and-a-half-hour drive in, if you take into consideration the fact that you had to keep to driving at 40 kph because of all the hairpin turns and the gravel road. I didn't want to make Grandad drive all that way. The mailman did the groceries for some people who live in that remote area and has been known to take someone around with him.

I'd forgotten until we were almost in Rai Valley that there wasn't cell phone reception there either, so I'd have to either hitch to Havelock to sort it and then stay at a DOC campsite, or go back through to Blenheim to stay with my aunty. I decided to go to Havelock; it was 4.00 p.m. by this stage and I was itching to keep going.

I got a mocha at one of the few stores in Rai Valley (mmm chocolate and coffee, yummy), and was waiting when another hitchhiker walked up to me and we started chatting away. Ash was a very relaxed guy and reminded me a bit of myself; the way he wasn't too stressed at how things were going to turn out; his motto was, just go with the flow.

Ash and I caught a ride together to Havelock with a chatty older British fella. Ash turned out to be an instructor at Outward Bound, which is an outdoor adventure school. He seemed so cruisy that when he said

I could come stay at his place up in Anakiwa, I thought it would just be a cool little shack or something.

We got to Havelock, which is the gateway town into the Marlborough sounds, and has a population of about 500 people. We cruised up the hill, and then had a race—he was running backwards of course, keeping it fair. We went down the road that went to Linkwater, which was the intersection for Kenepuru and Anakiwa. As we waited, he showed me how to sharpen a knife. He lit a fire—we both thought someone would drive past and lose their shit at us because of where we were—heated up some water, and had some miso soup that he was carrying. We waited a bit longer and one of the other instructors, Tui, who was obviously heading to the same place, picked us up.

When we got to his house on the Outward Bound campus, Ash gave me a homebrew beer, made me dinner and I played him a couple of songs on the guitar that I had written. He then gave me a tour of the campus, which was pristine, orderly and calming. Courses were due to start back up for the new year the next day, so it was rather empty, with a couple of instructors filtering back in after the holiday. Sitting right on the water as it was, with kayaks and bikes stacked up all around the place, it felt like an adventure campus, surrounded by classic New Zealand hill and native bush.

As we chatted with the instructors along the way, I realised that these were my kind of people: all wicked souls with cool 'living life' stories … and so relaxed. It's so hard to find relaxed people these days—properly relaxed, not stressing over money, who say, 'Yes, let's do it' instead of putting up barriers.

Coming back from the look around, we met Christie and her friend Jen. They had met overseas, and, like me, Jen was passing through. She was an attractive young American around my age; maybe a couple of years older, with blonde hair. She was maybe a little more reserved than I was.

Ash and Christie had that carefree confidence that drew you to them. Christie had done sports at an elite level and was solid and strong. Her sporting experience was something we had in common, so we had a small chat about what it was like to experience training and competition at that level.

We settled down for the evening in Ash and Christie's campus flat, and the mood was cheerful. There were only four of us, but the atmosphere was so friendly that I'm sure in the full swing of the year it would be a social hub for the instructors. They were enthusiastic about anything adventurous, which of course is what drew them to be instructors at an outdoors school in the first place, so they were definitely interested in the idea of a person in a wheelchair hitchhiking around solo with a backpack that was the size of him. It filled me with delight to be in this wonderful community with such a phenomenal energy.

Christie and I had a jam after dinner. I was nervous playing in front of people, but I knew the way to being a good singer and musician was confidence, so any chance I got I would really put myself in it. I got this kind of inspiration from that Jim Carrey movie, *Yes Man*. I liked that idea of saying yes, pretty much as habit and just putting yourself in it, and that was my attitude for these kinds of things. As a plus, everyone was interested in the electric travel guitar I'd brought with me, so it felt good knowing it didn't just end up being a dead weight.

It's amazing what happens when you relax and go with the flow.

Raetihi Bay: Grandad and Nan
5 January 2016

I HAD SLEPT OVER at Ash and Christie's that night—they're such cool people. Even though I'd said I wasn't going to have a shower—falling over backwards not to inconvenience them—I did. I got up and had breakfast with Jen: All-Bran, which I hadn't had since I was last training.

Anyone who has done some serious training at some stage would have had a run in with All-Bran—it's like eating carboard and you have to 'allow' time to eat it but it sure is good for your insides.

Jen was super sweet, and reminded me of the young girl who had been staying with Deb and Ian in Okarito Bay. We were hanging out by default in the morning, as both Ash and Christie were up and gone by the time we awoke, as it was their first day back instructing for the year, and they were out meeting their new students. I didn't mind one bit: I thought Jen was cute, and super friendly, so hanging out even by default was nice. We decided to go for a walk around Anakiwa Bay while I waited for a ride.

Eventually, we went and found Ash to say goodbye. While having a scone with them, I showed them how I got the pack on and off. One of the instructors showed me how to do a packflip to put the pack on—I figured I'd practice that on my own because I'd surely flip backwards, and I didn't need an audience for that!

At one point the night before while we were lounging, another instructor had come in for a chat. Later that night, he'd been skyping with a friend of his called Gemma, who, coincidence of coincidences, it turned out to be my basketball friend Gemma, whose mum, Karen, had taken me in! He'd mentioned that a guy in a wheelchair had hitchhiked into campus with one of the instructors, and Gemma just threw out the question, "What was his name?" Gemma and I hadn't been so much in touch while she was living in London, but I'm pretty sure Karen would have mentioned my adventure to her. Another example of how small the world can be.

Jen and I went for a walk down to the jetty, then sat and chatted. She had a card game similar to snap, and just as I thought I was mastering it, a camper pulled over up ahead. It turned out that Jen had spent Christmas with the people, so they gave me a ride to Linkwater, where I'd try get to Kenepuru to see Nana, my grandmother on Mum's side. They hadn't spoken much to Mum in those final years because of the alcohol, but I and another cousin were the golden grandchildren in their eyes, because of our achievements with sport. I always felt a little bad about that, because whenever Malachy or Faith spoke to them they always brought up the subject of our cousin or me.

Now to wait in the sun.

I waited about half an hour at a little gravel clearing on the side of the road, which wound onward into the bush. There was a big map sign of the Queen Charlotte and Kenepuru sounds, showing all the little towns around, and a few cars pulled over to look at that, so I got tricked a couple of times, thinking they were stopping for me. I decided to save myself the embarrassment and just wait until they rolled down a window to talk to me before I wheeled hopefully forward.

Then Sandra and her dog, Milly, who were from Christchurch, picked me up. They were going to Portage, and seeing as I didn't have reception to ring Nana and ask where I was going to get picked up (as I had forgotten), I went with them. Halfway there I remembered where I was supposed to be going, by which time I'd gotten phone service and rung Nana.

Yup, you guessed it; I'd passed it. Grandad didn't have his hearing aids in and couldn't hear me properly on the phone, so I got a coffee in Portage and waited for him. He crossed the sound in his own boat and picked me up from Portage. I think they were worried because they couldn't get hold of me and I kept not having service where I'd thought I would have. I jumped on the boat, chucked the bag over, and then pulled the chair in. It was such a nice day to go in the boat around the sounds. I love the water. I didn't mind the 20-minute sail over to their house in Raetihi Bay; although I'm not a skipper by any means, I do like boats and I'm comfortable in them.

Sandra and her husband were staying in Waitaria Bay, which was about an hour's drive from Portage, and since they'd been there her husband had to sail around to Portage to tie the yacht up each day, since all the moorings around the bay are privately owned. But Grandad had lived out here for 40 years, so he knew everyone.

I believe what goes around, comes around, and Sandra had been kind to me, so I asked Grandad if he knew if there were any moorings closer to Waitaria Bay that they could use. He asked around and found someone who was willing to let a stranger tie up their yacht at their mooring, so Sandra and her husband wouldn't have keep playing tag back and forth to pick each other up from the yacht. I rang Sandra and she seemed pretty stoked. They'd been so kind to me that I was glad to be able to return the favour.

We got back to Nana's with me still sitting in the boat as Grandad towed it from the beach up to the house because that was easier than putting the pack on and pushing, or transferring everything into the 4WD. Amazing that Grandad has still got the fitness to get the boat on and off the trailer and off the 4WD at eighty!

The rest of the afternoon I cruised around with Grandad, checking possum traps. It sounds a bit gruesome, but long after possums were introduced by the first European settlers to manage the snake population, their numbers grew to the extent where they themselves became a pest, as they kill the wildlife and native plants.

So they're trapped to ensure that native wildlife have a chance. I don't have it in me to be a hunter, but I can understand that things can become imbalanced in nature, especially when humans are involved.

As we went along, Grandad and I yarn to what seemed like every person that drove past. We had fresh-caught snapper for dinner—yum! That evening we watched the Kiwis win the cricket against Sri Lanka, and I gave Nana a game of Scrabble.

6 January 2016

I'D PLANNED TO WAKE EARLY, as Grandad and I were thinking of going fishing, but I slept in until 8.30 (which I was happy about, because I definitely had needed more sleep). I got up and had some breakfast, then Grandad and I went and checked the possum traps again while being stopped for a chat a few times by the locals who, of course, Grandad knew. No possums, so we went down to the lodge for coffees, then back up for another game of Scrabble.

While playing, I got a text from a guy in my basketball team, saying that there was training the next day at 5.30 P.M. That threw a spanner in the works because I'd planned to chill another day, and then head back with Neil, the mailman. The text had come in at 11.30 a.m., and the mailman shows up at Nana's at 12–12.30-ish—which didn't leave me much time to decide whether I'd ride in that day or go the next and just miss training. I decided to ride with the mailman and make training, seeing as we were going to a tournament in Australia a week later.

I stared out into the sounds, with the feeling that the adventure was coming to an end. I knew this was the last part of my hitchhiking test before I made my way home. Back to practice, back to sports, and back to the daily grind. Surrounded by beauty and calm, I made myself a promise, that one day I'd live somewhere like this. Someplace good for mind, body and soul. Although the thought of going back to my routine slightly dulled my spirit, I was intoxicated by this experience, and by the idea of doing this in the year to come: only next time, the world would be my playing field.

Grandad rang Neil to see if he had room in the postal van. He did, so I quickly packed my bag. I was a bit gutted that I didn't get another day with them.

It was about an hour-and-a-half drive around the sounds with Neil and then another forty-five minutes to Blenheim. I was quite tired so wasn't very chatty; he'd been running that route for so many years, and I don't think I was his first human 'delivery'. We just let each other be, and I was fine with that.

I needed food. Neil dropped me off at the i-Site in Blenheim, and I wheeled to a bar on the way out of town and waited twenty minutes for it to open at 4.00 p.m. I filled up on the best fish dish I've ever had: something called an orange roughy, fresh from the lake. It's a deep-sea fish that can live over 150 years—so not something that you often find in the supermarket.

After lunch, I wheeled further on to put the thumb out. The poor body had been hammered by the sun, and was out there again. I'd done up a sign saying Christchurch, and waited. A young fella picked me up in his 4WD and took me to Seddon, a tiny town just outside of Blenheim. He offered me a bourbon, but I think it would've put me to sleep. I sat in the sun for twenty minutes before an older bloke in a station wagon picked me up. He'd just bought an oven in Blenheim and was heading to Kaikoura, the halfway mark between Blenheim and Christchurch.

He dropped me off at the top of the hill in Kaikoura, and I pushed out of town and waited. I'd noticed there were a lot of shrugs, shaka hand signals and waves as people passed me. It was their way of letting me know that, even though they couldn't pick me up, there were no hard feelings. It was kind of comforting. This spot was beautiful and was such a nice spot to wait as the sun set. Then someone staying in South Bay in Kaikoura came over and said if I didn't end up getting a ride that he could help me back up the hill into Kaikoura, but I assured him I could push with the pack on my back up the hill, and shook his hand for the offer.

Then Marshall, a very chatty twenty-five-year-old from Nelson, picked me up. My gosh, he talked: about the dramas he was getting away from, about his girlfriend and ex-flatmates, about everything. No silence all the way from Kaikoura to Christchurch. I'm not one for small talk and gossip, so I just tried to interject some positivity into the conversation and add some stories of my own. It was cool to see he'd taken himself away from his troubles and just hit the road.

We got to Christchurch and I offered for him to stay at my house because he had no plan and it was 10.00 p.m., but I also gave him the name of a campsite and my number in case he got stuck—he seemed like he needed a break. He found a campsite and I didn't hear from him, which was good because it meant he was sorted.

I pushed from there to Josh and Ayla's because my phone was dead and my house was on the other side of town, but they must have been out on the road still, because they weren't home. So I wheeled to see if Ries, one of my best friends, was at his partner's house fifteen minutes away. Ries was an English guy I met through another friend, Tim, and who had come to New Zealand to be with his girlfriend. After they broke up, he found himself high and dry, not sure whether to stay or go back home. Tim had drafted me in to cheer him up after his relationship had fallen apart, and we went for a lad's night out. It was immediately clear that we had much in common, including our love of reckless fun.

I was in luck—he was there! So after charging my phone, I rang Malachy and he picked me up and took me home. I was showered and looking forward to sleep and not getting up early, and to have a nothing day, because even though it was an amazing journey and I planned to do it for years instead of weeks, I was shattered.

7 January 2016

WAKING UP FOR THE FIRST TIME in a couple of weeks without somewhere to be was an odd feeling. All I could think was that I couldn't wait to do this on a bigger scale (like the world) with unlimited time. I couldn't sit still, so went to the mall to get the photos developed, and then to the beach for a push along the path.

I tidied the house … back to reality. My friend Stephen and I met for a sushi lunch. I was brimming with my experiences but, again, not being much of a storyteller, I found it hard to convey the excitement and wonder of it all.

After I got back, I sat in the lounge, staring out the window and trying to adjust to sitting still, guitar in hand, and playing what came to my heart …

KIWI LAND
I'm heading back out on the road, my friends,
and I'm never coming back again.
I'm going to let it grab me by the hand,
and I'm going to let it consume my soul.
Hey, why don't you find yourself a new life, young boy.
Hey, won't you come back a man.
I see you,
and I know she sees me.
I see you,
and I know she sees me.
Now I'm back, and I don't know where I've been.
But I sure as hell know where I am now.
I've come back a changed man,
but I still don't know what to do.
Hey, why don't you find yourself a new life, young boy.
Hey, won't you come back a man.
I see you,
and I know she sees me.
I see you,
and I know she sees me.

THE GOODBYE ... AND THE START OF A NEW JOURNEY

IT TOOK ME A COUPLE OF WEEKS to settle down and get back ready for the working year after the small taste of freedom, excitement and experience from my couple weeks of hitchhiking. The year flew by and before you knew it was December again.

I was twenty-seven now. Around me my peers were buying houses, getting ready for or starting families, and moving up the ladder in their career—doing what seems to be the flow of life. I'd had my eyes open for so long, and here I was about to end my job to go travelling around the world with not enough money and no plan. Happiness seemed to be elusive, but it was so simple and right there ... so I had to say goodbye to the path I knew, to the people I knew, to every influence I knew and start in a place where I couldn't see what was in front of me. But

after my trial run around the south island the year before, the uncertainty didn't seem intimidating; instead, it was thrilling and full of promise. I'd done it before and aced it. There was no reason I couldn't do it again, in another country … on the other side of the world.

Finishing up a couple of weeks early to organise things was a great idea. As with last year's hitchhiking adventure, I didn't organise much, but seeing as I wasn't going to be under the rules of my own country anymore, I found out I needed more time. I had red tape to wrangle with, visas to apply for, and cheap flights to be booked. I'd managed to save NZ $15,000, but my rough plan was to be away at least a year, and I knew that was nowhere near enough to cover it, when you considered I was paying for flights, accommodation, food and anything and everything between. I tried not to be too detailed in my planning, because why rob myself of the thrill of being spontaneous?

Also, I had a Coldplay concert to go to.

It's a memory I'll never forget. I'd been to plenty of concerts, gigs and parties, but this Coldplay concert was beautiful. A total vibe of unity from the 43,000 people attending it. I felt a beautiful moment of sadness, as I'd chosen to sit in the wheelchair seats in the stadium, which were in between the seated people and the standing crowd. I was having a not-so-confident day, and I sat there, wishing that I hadn't succumbed to my nervousness when the concert helper had asked if we would like to sit in the wheelchair seats or be in the main part on the ground. I watched as people hugged, loved and danced with one another, knowing I never wanted to spectate again. No matter how afraid I was. It seemed too easy to sit there and look on from the sidelines. *Life* could be easy if you sat there and spectated, but for one moment of beauty, I'd give up any ease. I watched as this moment of beauty passed without me being part of it. *Never again.* This was a perfect reminder to happen two weeks out from me getting on the plane to England. In my mind, it made my purpose and intent real.

14 December 2016

I'm on the plane on my way to Heathrow airport in the first hour of the journey. I haven't been scared or excited (being a very in-the-moment type of person), and now having the freedom to not have any routine, plans or direction means that up until now it feels like I was working towards this freedom.

LOOKING OUT THE WINDOW was amazing, and I felt relaxed. I'd said goodbye to everyone (more in depth with some than others), telling them that I had no idea how long I'd be gone or where I'd be staying. Saying

UK Bound with ries

goodbye to Julie (you'll find out later who Julie was, but she was a lovely soul) at the airport wasn't easy. She was clearly upset, and I hate upsetting others, especially when I care deeply about them. I wanted to make sure people knew I was escaping to the unknown and that they might possibly not hear from me for a while. That act of separation stung, but I was too excited about this new quest that all I could see was what lay in front of me. Ries, who I was going to be spending the first five weeks with in England, also struggled with the goodbye to his partner.

The calipers I'd brought to support my legs were a pain already; not comfortable at all. Having an operation and spending three months in hospital to help me wander around a bit like Forrest Gump (but a much, much, much slower version and with crutches) turned out to be more of an around-the-house idea, rather than a two-twelve-hour-flights idea.

Although I must admit that even though it was super awkward to manoeuvre down the aisle with them to the toilet, it was so much less embarrassing than crawling along it for the inevitable toilet stops I'd need to make.

Sandwich, Kent

19 January 2017

I'D SPENT FIVE WEEKS with Ries. I had told him I'd have a white Christmas with him and his mum over in the UK. We spent that time in Sandwich in Kent, eating like hobbits and having pints down at the many local pubs. It was lovely and cosy, and on New Year's, we visited one and did the countdown. I sang karaoke … it was perfect (the experience, not the karaoke). I was too excited about what was to come to spend more than a few moments reflecting on the fact that a year ago I was well into my trial run, and that all the evidence was already pointing to the fact that I was capable, mentally and physically, of taking my wayward wheeling lark well beyond my home shores.

I was ready to start my solo part, and it had come around quick. I said goodbye to Ries and Sally, his mum, and caught a ride down to Brighton to where I would welcome my new adventure.

Somewhere along the line I'd come across this quote: *The tolerance of uncertainty is the prerequisite to succeeding.* It struck a deep chord inside me, and I was keenly aware that this was where I was heading in my life: towards uncertainty.

Ham sandwich, anyone?

Brighton

YOU CAN DO THIS. It is time to problem-solve and enjoy doing it. This is the time to show myself, no matter how much it all seems like an obstacle, that I can think my way through it. That I can adapt and be okay anywhere ... and still appreciate everything while I'm doing it.

I was telling myself this as I spent my first night in a motel in Brighton with absolutely no plan ... and now completely on my own with this giant backpack. The only thing I did know was I was flying out of Gatwick on 28 February, so I had another month and a bit before heading off to the States. What was I going to do?

I'll go for a push, that's what I'll do. Brighton was a stylish and progressive town overlooking the English Channel, with a crowded waterfront that would be swarming with tourists in the summer. World cuisine, eclectic markets, sidewalk cafes, funky haircuts and rainbow flags all over. Many people spilling into one small place. I wasn't in New Zealand anymore, that was certain.

I'd gone from the height of a southern summer to the depth of an English winter; quite a change, but I didn't mind. My excitement overruled any shivers I'd had at the definite nip in the air.

With my music being piped into my ears, I spent most of my time there pushing up and down and through the town with my little daypack with my book, my sweater and my charger so I could go to a coffee place at some stage and charge my phone and read. The daypack was a good idea, because anytime I carry something on my lap it is always falling off. It gave me more freedom, and that was what I was after.

20 January 2017

THE NEXT OBSTACLE was how I was going to survive. I knew I hadn't come away with enough money, but I'd had to go … I'd set this date when I was twenty-two—enough time to have finished my apprenticeship and work a year, six years to make sure I was ready. I took the leap, ready or not.

Busking with my guitar was on my bucket list. I couldn't have put myself out there much more than that! So, I went off down to a music store to buy a guitar. I understood it was a cost, but I had the money then to buy it, and soon wouldn't. At least that way if I ended up with nothing, I'd have something to make money with.

I'd brought my songbook with my originals too, so I came up with a set list and practiced it along with a few covers, though I enjoy playing original stuff more.

The guitar came with a bag with straps, so I could wheel around with it on my back, and I figured a way to attach it to my already-big backpack … so now it only weighed a trillion kilograms and took me a couple of practices to figure out how to get them both on and off my back.

22 January 2017

I'D BOOKED A WEEK IN THE HOSTEL in Brighton, the YHA, which was originally a hotel. It was such a cool hostel with a wicked vibe, strewn with interesting knickknacks and interesting people, who were milling about waiting on the 2.00 p.m. check-in time to roll by. The ground was littered with their huge backpacks, stuffed with whatever they'd decided they couldn't part with when leaving home.

I tried to make life easier on myself by booking places that didn't have steps and where I knew I could stay on the bottom floor or they had a lift, but with so many historical buildings, the UK wasn't a terribly accessible place. Most of the time I wound up staying in places that had stairs (which I'm totally cool with—I've always tried to adapt to the world around me instead of it having to adapt to me). That way I could be more independent.

I spent the day mooching—that's what they call wandering around. I'm sure that means something else back home. I particularly enjoyed seeing all the little bars and cafes, the winding alleyways that led to someplace new at each turn. So very hipster. I visited the pier, which featured an old-fashioned, cheesy, tourist-trap arcade and played a few games. If you didn't do that, you can't honestly say you've visited Brighton!

23 January 2017

DO PEOPLE LIKE MY SHOES or do I have funny feet, I found myself wondering as I wheeled around Brighton. I did stick out a bit because I didn't see many people in chairs around, probably because of the accessibility issues and hills, but I heard a chick say "nice kicks" (shoes apparently—ha ha) and my shoes were expensive: gold and white Timberlands that I'd snatched up for a deep discount, but nobody needed to know that! I went with the shoes theory.

I spent the day going into places to see if they needed volunteers. It would give me something to do and also I was hoping I'd end up with an offer for somewhere to crash so I wasn't spending all my money on accommodation, and I hadn't had any replies from the Workaway site I'd applied to yet. (Workaway is a cultural exchange/volunteer program where you volunteer four to five hours per day with someone. The work varies a lot from painting, labour, cooking, language skills or any kind of project that the host had going. In return, they feed you and give you a place to stay.)

No luck with volunteer work, probably because I had no references, and with my profile in my wheelchair I could understand that people wanted to know if I was going to require their energy or whether I could actually help—I was sure I'd figure something out.

24 January 2017

I MET UP WITH AN AUSTRALIAN GIRL, Mary, who was travelling on her own too. She had brown hair and a cute button face, with a steely stare she probably picked up as a self-defence mechanism while travelling solo. We became Brighton friends and hung out when we got bored at our respective hostels. So I ended up having a buddy for a week or so, which was cool because after the first week of mooching around, the city had lost its appeal and I'd wheeled all over Brighton.

I did have one adventure in a multi-storey nightclub, where I met a lovely brown-haired British lass who took me back to her flat—which was not flat at all, being about ten stairs up from the street and didn't have wheelchair access. Let's just say that the next morning's walk of shame turned out to be a bump-down-the-stairs of shame.

I'd also met up with a couple of basketball teams and did training with them. I had taken my basketball wheelchair with me, as I was still playing for the New Zealand national men's team and I wanted to play for a few teams in the different countries while I was travelling. I'd already made a few contacts online and was looking forward to playing.

I didn't end up travelling that much with the sports chair because it was so hard to travel freely with it. It was a pain trying to push my own chair while hauling around this huge backpack and guitar *and* this sports chair too. I'd even brought a basketball to train with, which was a bit over the top for someone travelling in a chair solo!

I caught Ubers to and from training, until I made friends, after which I got lifts from them. I trained every night that week with a different team, and it so felt good to be training—not that the pushing around the city wasn't good training.

25 January 2017

I'D BEEN WORKING ON MY GUITAR SKILLS, and while I wouldn't call myself a rock god, I was getting good enough to reasonably expect to busk without getting pelted with tomatoes. I made a wee sign and took the guitar out for a walk, finding the places that would work well acoustically and had crowds of people. At least I got that far. But if I had got that far, why not go that tiny bit more and play?

I was scared. I don't think the playing bothered me, it was the being in people's faces … *Tomorrow I'll do it,* I reasoned.

I didn't end up finding anywhere else to crash, so I had to decide whether to stay in Brighton another week. I'd found somewhere in London with some friends, Sile and Alex. They wouldn't be ready for me until the next weekend and I knew I'd seen and done everything there was to see and do in Brighton now. Well, as a traveller anyway. Although a well-travelled man through sport, I had no idea where to start or what to do next. I'd have loved to be in the country somewhere … but I booked another week at the hostel.

Still no replies from Workaway, darn it. It was amazing how many websites there were to help travellers. So I'd set up a couple of profiles on sites like that and Couchsurfing, an app where you can message people and crash at their house for a couple of nights. Also, I really needed to find a way of not spending so much money on places to stay. It was like applying for jobs, and I wasn't having much luck. I must have sent out forty messages to people around England, but only had a couple of responses saying that they weren't able to host me.

Just keep trying, I resolved, *I'm sure I will eventually get a 'yes'.*

26 January 2017

I REMINDED MYSELF that the purpose of the entire exercise was to get out there and face my uncertainties, and to overcome my mountains, whether physical or metaphorical, so I manned up and decided to go for it. I ticked busking off my bucket list.

As soon as I woke up, I got straight out of bed, grabbed my guitar and got a coffee. I was hoping the dozy mind from just waking up would stop me from talking myself out of it.

The hardest thing was just pulling the guitar out of the bag; playing wasn't hard. I originally went up to a shopping centre, but was warned that I would get told to move, so that scared me a little bit, but I still went to another spot and started playing.

Turns out I only made 70 pence (ha ha), so I'm not sure it counted. Sod's Law being what it was, I'd managed to pick the coldest day on record for Brighton, so I really didn't stay out long. I decided I just needed to beat 70 pence… How hard could that be?

> ***All experience has its worth, even if it's not the kind you intended to have.***
> Excerpt from my journal

27 January 2017

I WENT FOR TRAINING IN LITTLEHAMPTON, which was about an hour out of Brighton. I'd be training with a team that was more suited to my level of skills, which made me happy, because a few of the previous teams had been a bit grassroots, and less of a challenge. Although I'd been pretty lucky with cadging rides from friendly players, this time I ended up not being able to find someone who was able to, so I had to suck up paying for an Uber all the way there.

Littlehampton was a small seaside town; quite

picturesque, with the kind of sedate beauty you see on postcards. I wheeled around the seafront. The day was a bit grey; English weather, and all that. While wheeling down the seafront footpath, I stopped and spoke to an old man; nothing specific, just a bit of chit-chat. I had a few hours to kill before training, so I found a boutiquey-looking bookstore and had a look around and picked up a couple of books.

I love reading; a sentence in a book or a phrase from a stranger can make me happier than a year of working or all the money in the world can, and that's what I got from this philosophy book I picked up at this store today. It was a smallish book that could almost fit in your pocket (well, my pocket, which tends to be big). It had a worn brown cover, and although it was hard to read and didn't flow so nicely, it made me think. It was written in the 1940s and compared religion to science. While it didn't look like it had been a best seller, it sent me into thought.

28 January 2017

I MET UP WITH MARY and a guy from her hostel, and we went out for a drink. Then we headed to a nightclub—I love music and dancing, and people too. If I thought people hadn't seen someone out mooching in a chair before, they definitely hadn't seen someone out clubbing—not here, anyway. It was a positive vibe, though, and I got treated a bit like a celebrity.

I must say the night scene in Brighton had more appeal than it did in New Zealand. There were lots more people, for starters. The nightlife never ended, and the music was new and interesting. In New Zealand it can often be a mission in itself to find somewhere that is thronging with people, with big dance floors and music that never ended. In Brighton, the party went on and on.

Mary, Trevor and I danced the night away. During the night there came a point when Mary and I locked eyes on the dance floor—both of us feeling extra friendly after a couple of drinks. There was a fleeting moment when it felt as if my and Mary's skin gravitated towards each other. She gave me permission to take it further with her body language, but I let it pass. A moment later, the girl I was dancing with kissed me, and we continued our small romance throughout the night. We danced the night away and then ... sigh ... we all went sagely back to our rooms—separately.

2 February 2017

IT WAS MY LAST WEEK IN BRIGHTON before I headed off to London. I didn't spend much time in the hostel—I'd go out and get a coffee, listen to a band, go for a push and listen to music, and people watch (and people talk, ha ha).

I went to the cinema and the guy there was super-friendly and told me he'd handed in his notice and only had three days of work left, so he gave me a free ticket—people are awesome.

The weather had turned from cold and sunny to rainy, and I spent some time pushing in the rain. There's something nice about sitting in the rain … if you can let go of the fact you're going to be soaking wet.

I also played in a poker tournament, which was totally random but fun. It was just a small game, with a £20 buy-in, but it was still a bit intimidating because I'd only played online poker before, but I gave it a shot. It would've been nice if I could've won, but turns out there's a huge difference between playing poker online and in real life.

These were the locals I was up against. The casino was otherwise quite empty, as it was a Thursday evening, and there were only three tables playing poker; no one was watching. It was clear that they weren't about to let some stranger come into this poker tournament without a bit of a test. So they intimidated me. I'd be the first to admit that my skill level in poker is low, and I can't muster up a decent poker face even with a full beard. I quickly bombed out. I just lost the 20 quid, and my idea of making some money from poker went out the window with it.

4 February 2017

I went out for a goodbye drink with some people I had met – Hilde and company. I'd actually matched with Hilde on Tinder and was going stir crazy in the hostel, so she invited me out to the bar with work friends. They were very welcoming, even though I was a stranger. I also met two hardcase chicks—amusing and eccentric, for those of you who don't speak Kiwi—called Kate and Jenny, and hung out with them for a while in a local before I made the solo trip back to the hostel, listening to music and watching the rowdy people enjoying their Friday night, trawling from bar to bar.

The next day I'd be off to the bustle of London for the big-city experience.

> *Why I loved you, Brighton.*
> *People were holding hands and loving each other.*
> *People were embracing their individualism.*
> *I wandered down your beach late at night, watching the stars as I listened to your waves. The beach is endless and your alleys bustling with footsteps. Your beautiful sunsets were a perfect start to a new beginning for me.*

London

13 February 2017

LONDON, YOU GAVE ME NO DIRECTION; wonderfully lost, in awe of your rush. I could have spent years there and not seen everything. Time was gone before I even started counting.

Millions of people, and everyone on their own daily mission. I had a room I could stay in at Sile and her partner Alex's house. As much as I'm someone who is drawn more to wilderness, London left its mark, too. The transport mainly, probably because when I went out I was on public transport over half the time … buses, trains, undergrounds, ferries.

Two weeks in total and I felt that I hadn't even touched the surface of what London had to offer. Lively busking, everything moving, and people everywhere from all over the world. I spent my twenty-eighth birthday in London, and how wonderful it felt to be spending it in a new environment, wheeling around the streets, and on tubes and trains.

As with any major city, not everything was picturesque, but there was beauty all over, hidden away sometimes. My favourite experiences came from catching the tubes and trains—being enclosed with so many diversities, being able to watch people and interact with the busy

Saying Hi to Big Ben with Sile

people of London. I'd been getting wonderfully lost on numerous occasions, as some of the stops are wheelchair accessible to the street level, and some only in between different undergrounds, and it took me a while to figure out where and when to get off. Some days I spent three hours or so getting somewhere after being stuck going the wrong direction or going in a loop to catch a train that went somewhere I could get off... such an adventure. It was also partly because I just wanted to get on and wing it to my destination, which wasn't the fastest way to get there but it was the most fun.

I found myself sitting up in Sile's apartment, watching the snow come down outside, and finishing the song I had started writing in Brighton.

It's another rainy day in Brighton, my friends
and everyone understands,
and everyone is holding hands.
It's snowing here in London,
Everybody's head is down.
It's snowing here in London
and there is no one else around.

Oh, let me follow you.
Oh, let me follow you.
Oh, let me follow you.

I've missed another train and
I've caught, like, five buses.
Everyone is looking at me.
Everyone is causing a fuss.

Oh, let me follow you.
Oh, let me follow you.
Oh, let me follow you.
It's another rainy day in Brighton.
Everyone is holding hands.

Time doesn't go slowly in London, as you're pushed up to the pace it runs at, and I could feel that if I stayed for months, years could've passed in an instant. *London you amaze me, but I cannot stay.*

> **We travel, some of us forever, to seek other states, other lives, other souls.**
> Anaïs Nin, French-Cuban American diarist, essayist, novelist, and writer of short stories

14 February 2017

MIDWAY THROUGH MY SECOND MONTH in the UK, I found out that rental cars have the option to have hand controls put in them. That, to me, is *gold*; not only could I travel with ease, it also meant that for the time that I had the car rented, I'd have accommodation sorted as well—sleeping somewhere at a whim without any organising was my kind of travel. I was never afraid to sleep in the car; I usually found somewhere pleasant and private. I enjoyed the freedom of a moving house, and the knowledge that when I woke up I could just drive off. So I booked a rental for a week and would see where I ended up. To book the rental; they only required I let them know forty-eight hours before so that they could install the hand controls.

For my first stop, I thought I'd backtrack down to Sandwich, which was where I'd stayed with Ries and his mum for the five weeks, as I'd left my walking calipers down there because they were a pain to lug around and I hadn't planned on using them after the flight.

I got to the car rental company and filled all the paperwork out and went to do check the car out ... and realised there were no hand controls, even though I'd requested them with my order. Maybe they thought I didn't need them. At any rate, they were super-apologetic, and for the wait I ended up getting a free day's rental. I rang Sally and asked if I could stay the night, as I was still going to come down and get the calipers, but didn't end up leaving that day. So, another night with Sile and Alex and then made my way back down to Sandwich to pick up my calipers.

I'd spoken to one of my ex-girlfriends from back in New Zealand, as I wanted to meet her dad, who I knew was English and living in England. He seemed like someone I would love to meet. So Emma gave me the number for her dad, Nick, and we chatted. He offered for me to stay the next night, which was awesome because it's not like I had a plan. I'd been thinking I might head up to Scotland, but I knew it would take me a while because it was a long way from Sandwich.

| *Hitting the Road*
15 February 2017

UP EARLY AND ON THE ROAD, trying to figure what the speed limit was on the motorway ... so Google it was. I loved the motorway and the system of fast, medium and slow lanes, as opposed to the much narrower roads back home. There was no stopping for hours and hours. Also, thank goodness for cruise control, because the hand controls were literally just a couple of poles connected to the accelerator and brake. It sounds dodgy, but they were safe ...-ish. But holding down the accelerator with your thumb for five hours straight is not terribly comfortable.

Nick and Wendy were amazing. They were so

accommodating. We had some wine and whiskey, talked philosophies, chatted away and they told me places of interest in the north of the UK, Iona being one of them. It's a very spiritual place, Nick told me. Somewhere people go for peace. Now, that sounded exactly like something I was after, so there was a destination for me to head to the next day—or at least try.

It was a long drive from Eton to Oban. I didn't exactly have an endless amount of money; in fact, the opposite, so I was very aware that I couldn't spend money on this long trip and ferry rides. It sounded too nice to not go there, so at the very least I was going to drive up and check out Scotland, and if the ferry tickets were too expensive … they were too expensive.

| *Oban, Scotland*
16 February 2017

I WAS UP EARLY AND WAS FEELING GOOD even after the few wines and whiskeys last night. Nick and Wendy sent me off with a stomach full of English breakfast, which was amazing, and Nick and I exchanged details so I could let him know how the trip was going.

On the road ... the very long road up to Oban. I drove from 8.00 A.M. until 6.00 P.M. to make it up to beautiful Scotland, where I parked up in a forestry rest area and slept in the back of the car with the sound of the rain on the roof ... this is exactly what I'd wanted.

I did wake up paranoid in the night, though, because I'd parked near a bank in the rest area, and for some crazy reason I thought the rain was making me slip closer to the edge or that the bank might give way or something. I checked ... I was so far away from the bank—literally not even close. The tricks the mind can play!

17 February 2017

I GOT TO OBAN, expecting a small fishing town, somewhere lazy and sleepy, but it was buzzing ... well, compared to what I'd pictured, anyway. I did my daily routine of finding a coffee shop, charging my phone, reading and figuring out how to do whatever it was I was going to do. The coffee shop opened at 9.00 A.M. and the information centre at 10.00. Perfect. Enough time for a quick charge and a coffee.

The tickets for the ferries there weren't expensive, and I could even take the car across to the Isle of Mull, and just park it up somewhere with a nice view and sleep in it when I needed to. So that was accommodation sorted.

The more promising road on Iona

The Isle of Mull wasn't as small as I thought, though; it took me an hour and a bit to drive from where the ferry dropped me off, through the amazing and beautiful land made of nothing but volcanic rocks, to where the Iona ferry would take me across.

I could see the small island of Iona from when I got on the ferry, which cost just three pounds or something equally ridiculous. There only seemed to be two roads, so I wheeled down the one that looked more promising. It felt like this isle was as far from the other end of the earth as I could possibly go.

The lack of noise and the constant sound of the ocean breeze filled up my senses.

At the end of the road there was a sign which said IONA HOSTEL: VOTED BEST ECO-HOSTEL IN SCOTLAND. Well, firstly, I was surprised that there was a hostel at the end of the earth, and, secondly, I couldn't see it. Was being invisible also good for the environment?

Turned out it was hidden behind and down a grassy hill. I went down and waved to a woman who was at the door. She explained she was a volunteer there and showed me around. I said thanks. The fee was just 20 pounds a night, which, in the grand scheme of things, wasn't super expensive, but I had money on my mind.

I thought I'd just catch the ferry back to Mull and sleep in the car there instead, because Mull was nice too.

As I made my way out of the entrance to the hostel, I noticed a gate leading to a grassy field. The ground was cushiony soft and the track ran through a mountainous field of what felt like total freedom—the sound of the ocean and the soft breeze looking out from this island left me feeling like I had it all to myself at the end of the earth. This is what I'd envisioned my dream of peace to be, even as far back as that life-changing day when I'd first seen the Durdle Door on TV. I just lay there, looking up and out. It was so peaceful ... this was why I was travelling.

How could I not stay after that peaceful moment? I wheeled back down to the hostel and checked in. Then I wheeled down to the beach, parked up, jumped down onto the grass and spent the next hour or so watching the sunset, listening to the ocean and soaking it all in. Just being. After days of driving and taking ferries, here I was, wheeling around on this tiny isle of Iona! Everything was worth this moment.

That night, there were more people staying at the hostel than I thought there would be ... and again, it was magical. These people were all after the same thing. A young girl there, whose name was Iona (I know, crazy, right?), got out her fiddle, and there was a guitar sitting in the corner, so I snatched it up and we had a jam, providing some music for the other guests. A Scottish man and his partner bought a round of whiskies, and people began to dance.

At the end of the night, we all went up to the top of the grassy hill, and lay down under the clearest blanket of stars while Iona played the fiddle softly as we stared up into the night ….

Iona, the isle that is the reason for memory.

28 February 2017

THERE I WAS, BACK AT GATWICK AIRPORT. Off to America. I'd had a smashing time in the UK, and I was eager to move on to the next chapter, being on my own in an entirely new environment.

Carrying everything wasn't as hard as I thought. I used my basketball wheelchair as a trolley for my backpack and threw my guitar on my back. I'm always early to the airport, as I hate rushing. I have a bladder that's the opposite of a camel's hump, so I have to go to the toilet just before I get on the plane, and my worst fear is being late and then having to go to the toilet and hearing: 'Could a Mr. Eamon Wood make his way to the gate, please.' That would mean I had to get on the plane and to my seat while everyone watches from their seat … Nightmare-ish stuff.

The travel gods were with me; I avoided all that and got on the plane. *America here I come.*

STARTING A NEW CHAPTER IN AMERICA

I LEARNT A LOT FROM MY TRAVELS IN AMERICA. Because of the media, the political climate, and my being on the other side of the world in New Zealand, I'd subconsciously formed a wrong opinion of this wonderful country. Some of us have different accents and different cultures and live in totally different climates, but one thing has become apparent to me, and that is that ultimately we are all the same. Our views can differ slightly, but sometimes we're more united than it seems. Some people have their protective barriers higher than others, but their intent is the same as yours. There's hope yet. Keep being beautiful.

Newark, New Jersey

28 February 2017

FLYING INTO NEWARK, New Jersey, to start my American adventure was a shock to my system. I knew no one there, had no plans, and it was a true test of my ability to adapt. My first fluster was pushing around in circles around the airport trying to find a payphone that worked, and I must have looked a bit silly as I pushed my basketball chair, big backpack and guitar around past the same people over and over.

Something as small as using a phone changes from one country to the next. It didn't help that people there didn't have any time for you and were abrupt. If America was going to be like that, I thought, maybe I should just get back on the plane and head back. Luckily, it wasn't, but it took me a week to figure that out.

My big plan was to buy a van, travel all over the States with my basketball chair and my guitar, play ball, play guitar out of the back and sleep in the van. That plan came crashing down after a few days of trying to buy a vehicle – the process was too complicated. I was sitting in the hotel in Newark trying to figure it all out, knowing that I only had a few thousand dollars to last me three months, before I was off to Spain …. How the hell was I going to do that?

Dry the tears and carry on

I got further flustered by Newark, with my heart breaking that day. I arrived at this cheap motel I'd booked at the airport. When I got there, the reception staff stood behind a screen of bullet-proof glass and spoke to me like I was a criminal. Then, as I pushed around the neighbourhood and went into a Dunkin' Donuts for a coffee, I felt a strange body language radiating from the people there, silently saying, 'this is no place for you, mate', as I was the only white person I saw. But it might have just been a touch of cultural dissonance.

Nonetheless, the experience hurt me, as I lived in a fantasy land where everyone treats everyone how they would like to be treated—that a human is a human; when we look at each other we see other humans and not races or social statuses.

Now, I'm sure I'd be better able to roll with punches like that, but at the time my naivete got the better of me. I cried in my motel room over how people were treating each other, people pushing in front of people, no one helping one another. And were there really places still segregated? Of course, I'm not stupid, and knew what the world was like—but I really didn't know. *Imagine what it was like in a third world country,* I thought to myself.

America is always portrayed as the land of the free and the home of the brave, a place I'm sure many people from the third world travel to in hopes of making their dreams come true. And if this is what it can feel like in a 'first world' country, maybe I knew nothing. I'd even been to countries that are considered third world playing tennis, but I realise now that the reality was shielded from us athletes. I felt like a child having his innocence blanket ripped from him.

Like a lot of people, I was dwarfed by the problem and was desperate to leave for the sake of my positivity. So I left, ashamed for letting the thought go, took an Uber down to Philadelphia and booked a week in a hostel there. This wasn't cheap either, as I had my basketball chair and all my stuff, so it had to be a UberX, which is a bigger vehicle like a van or station wagon.

First off, I had to find a way to store my basketball chair with someone, as there was no way I was going to be able to afford to Uber everywhere, and I planned to hitchhike now. Secondly, I really needed just one person to get back to me from the Workaway site. Where were the jobs I'd been expecting?

| *Philadelphia, Pennsylvania*
4 March 2017

I ARRIVED AWKWARDLY in my UberX with all my stuff, stumbling through the hostel entrance, needing help with the doors, trying to get my basketball chair through; I have to take both wheels off, otherwise the camber makes it too wide. So I had to balance the wheels, guitar and bag while trying to do this. Luckily, the Uber guy saw me struggling and came to the rescue. It felt awkward as, like I mentioned before, most hostels have their common room near the reception, and here was the same. The last thing I needed was so many pairs of eyes on me.

I made myself known and tried to mingle around the hostel after putting my stuff on the bunk bed and my basketball chair into a storage room. The staff turned out to be lively and every second day they ran a pub crawl, so it's safe to say I got caught up in this and partied a couple of nights away. That partying remained one of my indelible memories from that leg of my journey. By day I headed out with someone else who was staying at the hostel. Many of the guests were Americans from different parts of the country.

One day, I and another guy from Boston went looking for a Philly cheese steak—a bread roll with thin pieces of beef steak and that special ingredient: Cheez Whiz. Another day, a Canadian named Mike and I went in search of the famous 'Rocky' steps and I filmed him running up the stairs and doing the jumping fists in the air at the top … like a million other tourists before us.

Amazingly, another Kiwi, Mitch, showed up to the hostel, the only one I met in all my months of travelling around. As we started talking, a couple of people stood around with confused looks on their faces as my and Mitch's filter came right off and our 'twangs' came out in to the light while we spun a yarn—not worrying about those mixed up 'i's and 'e's. An American standing in the conversation circle said he had no idea what we were talking about.

Another day, while wheeling through the city, I came across a rehabilitation centre for people with spinal injuries and such. So I wheeled in to meet some patients and came across a staff member in a wheelchair. We sat around and talked awhile about sport, and what the main reasons were that saw people ending up in the rehab hospital. To my surprise, being shot was one of the main reasons.

When it comes to being in a wheelchair, I'm a veteran, someone who knows the ins and outs, and it's second nature to me, so even back in Christchurch I would pop into the spinal unit and wheel around, talking to people. Right after a life-changing accident like losing a basic body function that you previously took for granted, you can place a lot of focus on what you've just lost. So I like to go in there and show patients through my stories and connections that there are a lot of positive aspects

to their new life that they can learn to focus attention on and find purpose.

I asked the guy about basketball and if there were teams in the local area and he gave me a contact. Safe to say that I organized to go along to a training session pretty quickly, trying to pull myself away from the partying a bit. Uber were getting a lot of business from me, as I often failed to find a train or someone going that way. I turned up to training and pushed around, constantly looking for a level a little higher than what I was finding. But still it was fun to network and sweat a little.

One thing that constantly took up space in my brain was money: how much I had and how much I'd been spending. I was down to only a few thousand dollars after my time in England, and that $15,000 I'd had at the start was in New Zealand dollars; after you convert that to pounds or American dollars, it's almost half that. I was burning money, about to be stuck with none. I knew I needed to change my style of travelling, and quick.

I remember arriving in the US, when the lady at border control looked at me and very sternly said, "Now, you know you can't work here, don't you?" and I replied with, "Of course!" telling her my plan to buy a van and travel around playing basketball. And that *had* been the plan, to do that great American road trip and have all my stuff conveniently in the back of a cheap van, where I could sleep, too. But after that first experience in New Jersey, trying to buy the van, and discovering how difficult it was compared to buying a car in Australia or New Zealand where you can just outright buy a car, this dream all came to a crashing halt. In the US you had to get the car picked up by a company and then insured before you drove it, and there were all these other bureaucratic walls. With my cash dwindling, I really explored every idea to make money to survive. I was looking for cash jobs —which was illegal … I know!

Eventually, after lots and lots of messaging, I did get a response on Workaway, and that was from Priscilla in Pennsylvania. She didn't specify the work; she just told me that we would figure it out when I arrived. That sounded reasonable to me.

I was grateful that she'd given me the shot at proving that the wheelchair wouldn't stop me from going into a house with stairs or doing whatever work that they had for me. I would figure a way out, but I just needed someone to give me a chance so I could get a reference saying that the chair wasn't a problem.

So, after a great week of good vibes and people in the hostel in Philly, I caught a train down to Harrisburg, Pennsylvania. In retrospect, I should have caught a train from Newark to Philly after I experienced how easy it was to catch the train.

| *Locust Gap, Pennsylvania*
10 March 2017

I SPENT THE NEXT TWO WEEKS IN LOCUST GAP, a community an hour out of Harrisburg, with a population of 388 people. It was the perfect for me to adjust to America, and also to have the time to adjust my strategy for the rest of my trip. I was staying in a converted church, a creative haven where I was helping paint radiators for my work. A massive snowstorm hit

Pennsylvania, with snow settling up to the height of a car, so we were stuck inside for a few days. It's safe to say I was itching to get out and explore and feel that chilling air. On St. Paddy's day, the fire brigade was holding a function for the locals, so I just shovelled myself a pathway in the snow and made it over to this function.

You know those western movies where the new gun in town walks in through those swing doors and everyone in the bar stops what they're doing, turns their heads and looks around? Yeah, it was like that. A moment later they turned back to their business.

Being a Kiwi is a bit of a novelty and it seemed so especially here, as there were some people who had never even met someone from another country before, which totally blew my mind.

Saint Augustine, Florida
30th March 2017

AFTER TWO WEEKS, I was ready to make my way to another state. I'd thrown out some emails on Workaway, and a few people had got back to me. Thinking I should take a linear direction to try and see as much along the way as possible, I decided to go down to Florida.

Flying was the cheapest way this time around, so I flew down into Orlando, leaving my basketball chair up in the church with Priscilla, which was an amazing weight off my travelling shoulders, seeing as I wasn't going to be doing the basketball tour I originally thought, thanks to the van snafu. Without the van, travelling around the country by bus, hitchhiking, planes, hosts' cars and trains would be a nightmare and more expensive. There was no option that I could be a vagabond on a budget with a basketball chair.

My travelling plan was to finally be able to embrace my go-with-the-flow attitude, to go anywhere, anytime, at the whim of my heart's desire without it affecting anyone in a negative way. I was starting to flow—each day I was getting more confident that life was going to provide me with a positive experience regardless of the fact that it might be 11:00 P.M. and I was in a new city and had nowhere to stay.

Heidi, me, and the Dalai Lama

Since I left Ries back in Sandwich, I'd completely fallen off grid. I hadn't bought a sim card so I relied on Wi-Fi wherever I could find it. I was sticking to this romantic off-the-grid idea; no way anyone could contact me. Maybe it was an idea that needed some refining as I wasn't talking to anyone back home apart from Julie when I could, and even then I hadn't made much time for her, which I am not proud of; I hadn't even started a Facebook page or a blog about my travels yet.

I arrived in Orlando that night, having to find a way to Saint Augustine the next day to meet with my next Workaway host. I booked the cheapest hostel room I could find. I had no idea how to get there, but I got up early and watched an amazing sunrise over the water before setting off to hitchhike to my new assignment.

The transition from Pennsylvania snow to Florida heat was a shock, especially now that I was pushing a distance with my big backpack. I'd been pushing along the road because I'd run out of footpath, and … look at that, I found a train station!

I caught a train up to Palatka, a small city in Putnam County, and was trying to hitchhike the rest of the way at 7:00 P.M. It was still light out, with another hour to sunset, but I wasn't having much luck and wondering why. Just then, a young man called Joseph and his aunty shouted across the road from their rental car and asked if

I needed a ride …. He told me it was illegal to hitchhike in Florida, but he'd seen me on the train. So he picked up his first ever hitchhiker that day.

Saint Augustine; what a memory it gave me. Firstly, Venessa, Heidi (her daughter) and Kim (Venessa's friend down the road) were so inviting. The fact that people could welcome into their homes—someone they had never met—gave me the belief in the world that I needed and had been searching for. To trust and love without expecting anything in return.

I helped Venessa around the house and did some gardening. One night we went out to see the Saint Augustine nightlife. We listened to some music at one of the local bars and then Venessa went home, and I carried on into the night, meeting new people and dancing. In the early hours of the morning, I hitchhiked back to Venessa's, which was about a 40-minute or so walk from the city. It was a cool experience.

Venessa is a sign language interpreter because Heidi is deaf, so I was so happy to be learning another language. I learnt a lot about sign language, and by the end I could at least spell the words and was capable of having a caveman conversation … whatever the medium, I was glad that I was capable of communicating simply with someone.

We all meet those people who influence us majorly at

Easy riding with Jan

some point of our lives. This person has something that you aspire to learn, or gives you a perspective that you couldn't have seen before. Jan, a 21-year-old guy from Germany, was the person I'd met on my travels who had influenced me the most so far.

Jan was doing a similar work exchange with Kim, so we would pop over to each other's place, have bonfires, sing, and exchange our stories and true thoughts. We even went busking together in Saint Augustine.

Everyone I meet has an influence on me, but Jan was a projection of how I wanted to be. I went travelling to let go, to really let go. To become as free as I possibly could, free from what I think of myself, others and everything else. To rid myself of the negativity that fills the mind. To really expand my awareness of my surroundings on a broader scale than just my life and the city I work and live in. To finally accept my place, and start going with whatever flow I was meant to be flowing with.

Jan had let go; he was sharing his love with everyone, smiling at everyone, and floating down the current of life. He had put himself out to the world a couple of years earlier, cycling down the west coast of the States from Vancouver to San Francisco. Along with all his other amazing stories and lessons, Jan seemed free, and that's the direction I was trying to head.

One particular experience stood out for me, though—our wander over to Vilano Beach. It must have been an hour's bike ride/push from Venessa's to Vilano, and between Vilano and Saint Augustine there's an intercoastal bridge with a high arch to allow boats to go under—probably ten minutes to cross on the bike.

As soon as we started up the bridge, a powerful thunderstorm hit out of nowhere and this wall of rain hit us, me in my singlet and Jan carrying the guitar. The power of nature was beautiful and a reminder of what true power is—the huge cracks of the thunder right above us and the rain hammering us. My awe overrode any self-preserving warnings in my head about the possibility of getting myself Darwinned by lightning; still, I was careful not to touch the metal side rail of the bridge. If you haven't gone out in a thunder or rainstorm, then I recommend it. There's no reason to be afraid of water. So much of our world is made up of water, and maybe one day we may not have this precious element so readily available …. It's a refreshing awakening.

As soon as we got down the other side of the bridge, the dark clouds left as quickly as they had come and the sun was shining. Within half an hour I was dry again.

> *PUSH YOURSELF, PUSH PAST WHAT YOU THINK YOU CAN DO, AND THEN KNOW YOU'RE CAPABLE OF ANYTHING.*
>
> Excerpt from my journal

| *Key West, Florida*

10 April 2017

I'M NOT SOMEONE WHO PLANS THINGS. I love to go with the flow and follow the opportunities as they arise, so when someone in Saint Augustine told me about the celebration of the sunset in Key West, the southern-most point in the USA, it sold me on the idea of going down. I mean, could there be anything more worth celebrating than the celestial body that provides life to us on earth?

Venessa suggested that I go down with Heidi to visit and stay with Heidi's father, John. We caught the famous Greyhound bus down together to West Palm Beach, not far out of Miami.

John was awesome—seventy years young, full of life and very chilled. We got on well, played music and philosophised the days away. Heidi was also going to go visit her brother, Edward, who was also in a chair and lived in Miami.

I had decided in those few days that I was going to hitchhike down to Key West from Miami, and instead of taking that monstrous backpack, I left it at John's along with my guitar, only taking a small CamelBak hydration pack with a charger, jacket, book and a couple of other small things.

Little did I know that when I got to Edward's, someone was going to tell me about a cycleway going pretty much the whole 160 miles (257 Km) from Miami to Key West. *Well, why not push down,* I thought. I love the sun, I love adventure, and most of all, I love to push myself physically, not only because I know the wheelchair wouldn't slow me down, but because exercise is the perfect anti-depressant. The biggest high you will get is from pushing your body and mind past what you think it might be capable of to get to a point where you have to talk to your body to keep it moving, with sweat running into your eyes and the burn of your muscles, each breath being of value … I live for that feeling.

If you're ever struggling with anything in life, go for a run, swim, push, bike or anything where you can exhaust yourself physically and bring you back to your simplest appreciations – your breath, your heartbeat—and you have pushed so hard that you only have enough energy to be in the moment. The valuable energy that you have at that moment is spent on the processes of the now, and only positivity can fill your mind.

It was 3.00 p.m. by the time I had decided to push down, so Edward invited me to stay the night. Pushing starts tomorrow, then.

160 Miles of Freedom

Day 1 - *The sun battle*

BECAUSE I HADN'T PLANNED ANYTHING, I hadn't thought of what I should pack, where I should stay, or how or where the path was. I just literally left where I had been staying, went and got a coffee and started pushing—hopefully in the right direction.

A long push begins

Stopping off to pump up my tyres at a bike shop, I started on the path which was slowly turning from Miami city to a seemingly endless backroad. I loved the physical push, but it was hot and I knew I was getting sunburnt, so had to stop off and buy a hat. Twenty or so miles later, after enduring the heat, drinking all the water from my CamelBak, and being sticky and burnt, I found a hostel that someone had recommended. Thankfully, they had room, because I needed to tend to my burns with some aloe vera from the hostel garden and refuel for the next day.

Day 2–3

WHAT A DISTANCE, what an experience: two days merged into one. Having been told there was no space for pushing on the road between Florida City and Key Largo, I decided that I would bus to Key Largo (the start of the Florida Keys), which was about twenty miles away.

It was another day of extreme sun, but I wore a t-shirt and used a lot of sunblock to try to recover. My experiences the day before meant that I had to manage myself today with the sun. I pushed and pushed. I started at about 9.00 A.M. and stopped around 1.00 P.M. to have lunch, and then kept pushing. At around the twenty-mile mark, I started to look for places to stay the night, preferably a hostel or something cheap. This was around 3.00 p.m. No such luck, and I got a bit off the main track and was now wheeling on the road, thumb out, to hitch a ride back to the main road where there was a path.

I got a ride with Rocky, Liinci and their newborn daughter, and hung out with them for a little while down at a beach. They showed me some local spots that might not be so busy with this crazy traffic of people, where I could possibly sneak in and sleep on the beach for the night. It was around 4.00 p.m. when they dropped me off at a beach place, but it was busy and I still felt like pushing. So I pushed and kept getting further, and it kept getting later … until it was dark and I was still pushing and hadn't found somewhere to stay for the night.

I asked around, but everywhere was booked out. Maybe I should have picked a weekend that wasn't spring break *and* Easter weekend!

Pushing over the bridges during the day was okay; I was close to the cars but I knew they could see me, but I came to a bridge at about 10.00 p.m., and had luckily accidently packed my head torch, so I had that on while pushing, otherwise I would have probably wheeled straight into the ocean. This was a bridge with a big arch to allow boats to go under and I asked people who were fishing there if I could catch a ride over – no response.

I tried hitchhiking over – no response. They literally looked at me like a criminal and gave me that side look, the kind of look that someone might give a drug addict on the street asking for money. Then they pretended I wasn't there. I had to laugh. Firstly I was like, "Oh, man, not even a response" and felt a little irritated, but the next day I would have laughed.

I decided I should wait until the early hours of the morning when traffic died down. At this stage I was pretty keen on having a rest and sleeping, but there was nowhere. The grass was full of beady-eyed spiders, so that was out. I wheeled down a bank (unknowingly through some cactus plants) and chilled in the bush for some sleep in my chair. I tried to sleep, but I kept hearing sounds and wasn't sure what was hiding in the bush, so out of desperation of trying to find somewhere to rest, I pushed over a bridge with my headlamp facing backwards to warn oncoming traffic, pushing as fast as I could, being prepared to dodge cars and to be yelled at.

I made it and kept pushing. Around 1.00 A.M. I started singing, because there were no people around and this endless path was making me insane. 'I push for days and days,' I kept singing for some reason. At about 2.00 a.m., I decided to sleep on this pedestrian bridge that runs along the main car bridge. Amazingly, there were people fishing in the dark and a couple of what looked like homeless people. I acknowledged them, though not very boldly, given my previous experience with the fishermen up the way. And to be honest. By then *I* was the one looking like I could have some mental health issues at this point, and people were avoiding my gaze. It was pitch black on this weird bridge that seemed like a place that no one should be.

Oddly enough, I felt safe; I actually suspected people were more scared of me in this situation. You can kind of sense when someone doesn't want to talk to you or are trying to avoid a situation where they talk to you. I sometimes get this in the chair, but with the beard and the darkness, this was amplified for sure.

Whatever. I jumped out of my chair, put my warm jacket on, used my backpack as a pillow and lay down to try and sleep under the moon in this concrete island in the middle of the ocean with the wind whipping all around.

After a couple hours of sleep … you guessed it; I went back to pushing. At around five, I fell asleep on the steps of a motel, waiting for it to open at eight. I waited … and then was told there was no room. My eyes were popping out of my head and my body was feeling like it had just pushed fifty miles (which it had).

I saw a bus go by and was so tired and hungry that I began to berate myself for choosing one of the busiest weekends of Florida's year. That's what happens when you just take a plunge and go. I forgave myself.

I decided to catch a bus back up to Edward's in Miami. Wow, watching the bus drive for a couple of hours and seeing how far I had pushed was cool. It hadn't seemed that far because I wasn't focused on the destination—I had just kept pushing.

Edward was awesome and let me stay so I could have a shower and wash off the fifty miles of sweat, eat, sleep and continue in a couple of days when Easter was over.

Day 4 – Rested, ready and eager to get back pushing

I WAS RESTED AND REALISED how much I missed being out on my own in the unknown. I caught a bus back down to Marathon, which was where I had caught the bus from to come back up.

I met up with Marta, who is a friend through a friend. Marta was the typical olive-skinned Italian, and was working for her stay at the hostel (was more of a cottage set up as a hostel). These days it would probably be an Airbnb, but back then there was no such thing. The owners were on holiday and there were just a couple of travellers keeping the place running. Marta snuck me in and gave me a bed; just a nice person helping me out for the night.

Day 5 – A night under the stars

I WAS UP BEFORE EIGHT to start pushing again. I pushed about thirty-two miles and had to try to hitchhike across a seven-mile-long bridge before I found somewhere to stay—another campsite. I managed to talk the price down by 20%, seeing as I was getting a tent site but was going to sleep outside. I always appreciate a place to shower and charge my phone, have a place to chill and refuel.

That night I got out of my chair and slept on a park bench under the stars. What a beautiful night ... except for the millions of mosquitos. I slept wearing my jacket backwards with the hood over the front of my face and my hands tucked in—genius! It stopped the bites, anyway. (Maybe not something to do if you want to look cool, though).

Day 6 – The final destination: Key West

I KNEW I'D MAKE IT to the southern-most point of the USA today. I got up early and pushed along the road, over bridges and through towns. From around eight in the morning until noon, I was pushing—not as long as the other days. I had come 120 miles or so miles ... now for the last stretch.

I really did enjoy the sun and having my music in.

Along the way, people in stores and on the street would come up and say that they saw me wheeling along the road or wherever. There was pretty much no one on this path down the Keys so I stuck out more than I usually would.

Finally, I made it. I was so sweaty that my clothes were drenched, so I had to find some showers. I found a community pool on a rooftop, which was awesome. There were only locals there. I got to cool down and refresh so that I could go celebrate the sunset with the rest of the tourists of Key West.

After going into one of the three hundred bars in Key West to listen to some music, I managed to get mistaken for a homeless man—again. I'd been wheeling down to the beach and someone came running from across the street up to me and asked if I needed any money. Rather than take offence, I acknowledged my scruffy appearance inwardly, and answered nicely, "Nah, it's all good—thank you though. I'm actually not homeless." Then I ruined the effect by stumbling a bit as I said, "I actually don't have a home, though," as he stood there longer than he thought he would.

I caught up with Aramis, who I had connected with via the Couchsurfing website, and whose houseboat I'd be bunking on for the night. Then it was down to Mallory Square, where I watched the performers and looked out across the ocean at the sunset and said thank you.

Thank you for teaching me that I don't need much, that things will work out even if I have to sleep outside. That I can journey as long and as far as I like if I appreciate the journey. That the destination is just a milestone of a start, the start of a bigger journey.

| *Lafayette, Louisiana*
25 April 2017

SO, AFTER THE WEEK I SPENT on my Key West adventure, and getting back to John's house in West Palm, I decided to give away my backpack, sleeping bag and tent. For one, I didn't need it as much as I thought I would have—and in fact, I enjoyed having less.

Secondly, I wanted to teach myself to become more of an expansive soul, sharing my love and giving without intent of receiving.

It's funny, because the year before I came travelling, I'd got a loan to get all this gear which had cost me around NZ $2,000 (about US $1,200), and now I was giving it away. So I set up a video, put it up online for anyone who might need a hand starting an adventure, and said I was giving it away.

My next Workaway stop was in Lafayette, Louisiana, with Trent and Linni. I caught a twenty-two-hour bus ride to Lafayette. It was a long ride with interesting people along the way. A skinny young white guy with dreadlocks, who had just started learning about permaculture, exchanged books with me. He gave me his Bhagavad Gita, which meant a lot to us both. At about one or so in the morning, at one of the bus stations, a lady was moved by the spirit to begin shouting that Jesus would heal me. I tried not to encourage her, but said thank you and carried on.

Arriving in Lafayette at five in the morning and not wanting to wake up Linni and Trent, I waited there a couple of hours. I met a dude who was homeless and took him out for a classy Burger King breakfast, gave him my spare pair of corded headphones, and wished him luck on finding a home and work. I still had my Bluetooth headphones, which I used unless my batteries died. I think I gave them to him because he asked.

The encounter was memorable for me; one of the most memorable moments along my travels. I never told anyone about it because it was such a nice moment and I didn't want to justify it or take anything away from it.

I'd met him at the bus station, just waiting for time to magically pass, when he approached me. He was an African-American fella, a detail I wouldn't usually mention, but in America I knew he would have been treated differently approaching strangers. I got the sense that he was just someone who was stuck in the system, but trying to get out—possibly with some mental health issues.

I was having a chat with him, and then my bladder did its thing and I said I needed to go use the public toilet, which was only about 20–30 metres away in the station. It was still dark and around 5.30-6.00 A.M. I started to put my big backpack on with the guitar strapped to it and he said, "Yo, man, I got you; I'll look after it."

"Sweet," I said, "I'll be back in five minutes." Some people would say that that wasn't very street smart, leaving thousands of dollars of gear with someone who had no possessions in his life apart from his clothes and the bike he was on and was at rock bottom. But the look on his face when I didn't hesitate with trusting him with all my stuff was worth a lot more than all my current possessions. I remembered, too, that only a week ago I was in his position, when I was the one people were a little bit afraid of approaching at early hours in the morning on the bridge I slept on.

I came back from the toilets, and I knew that this was a positive moment in his day—maybe the first that he'd had in a while. Not positive as in being given money off the street, but positive as in being treated like a human being, as an equal. My gear was still there.

If you remember, I'd just put up that video online about giving my stuff away anyway. Looking back now, I question why I didn't give all my stuff to him. But at the time it didn't feel right—plus I hadn't sorted through what I was going to keep in the bag to transfer to the small CamelBak.

How amazing is it when you have no plan and then you arrive on the exact weekend Lafayette is having an international music festival. Trent and Linni were an alternative type of couple, married since college. Trent was white haired and soft spoken and Linni was the one with the voice and personality. We all went out. The town was closed off and full of stages and we listened to Cajun music and music from all over the world. I remember seeing this young girl doing this weird dance, swinging her arms and hips in a way that was almost an optical

illusion. I thought, *What is this?* It was until I was back from travelling that learned that all the kids were doing it, and they called it "flossing". So great.

I was rushing now. I only stayed a week and only had a few weeks left in the States. Where did these three months go? I felt like I hadn't even touched a fraction of the USA. I could definitely have spent a while longer in Lafayette, helping with the gardening and then swimming in their pool in the afternoons, or kayaking down the bayou behind their house. But it was time to go and cram in some more.

Austin, Texas
4th May 2017

I HAD BEEN IN CONTACT WITH A FRIEND of someone back home, John, who was in Texas. He had posted on Facebook, asking if anyone had somewhere for me to crash, and another friend, Chris, got back to him. If there's one thing that I can take away from travelling, it's that people are awesome, and that it has encouraged me to be awesome back to everyone.

I caught a train from Louisiana to Austin, Texas. I spent a night sleeping in a train station, getting dead arms multiple times, and exploring San Antonio at two in the morning rather than sleep in the train station. Nothing exciting happened, unfortunately, apart from finding myself a good American burger.

At this point, meeting with strangers, spending time and staying with them for a night, a few nights or a week was becoming normal. Chris was awesome. I had the feeling that he was secretly an eccentric genius and I wouldn't have been surprised if I ended up seeing him on the cover of some grand magazine somewhere, for whatever his tech company did.

We jammed out on the guitars, he helped me write a song and we hung out like it was a boys' weekend while his partner was away. He took me out for dinner at a

Busking in Austin

couple of places, and one night he drove me into the city and dropped me off and ordered me to have fun and drove off. There I was, stranded in the city in the middle of this street festival thing that was going on. Needless to say, I took full advantage and found myself wheeling back to his house at 4.00 a.m. after another night of new faces, dancefloors and sharing my travelling story with friendly strangers.

My American song

Well, I have been trying to make my way around
where the voices are so loud.
I went busking in Saint Augustine
where I spent all my money on caffeine.
I learnt this rhythm in Philly
where they have cheesesteaks and really good weed.
We're different but the same,
coming from the same place.
America, what have you done to me?
America, the land of the free.
America, what have you done to me?
America, everyone has treated me so beautifully.
Austin is not all cowboys and westerns.
It even has a Google building
and I spent $31.70 on going up the Empire State Building,

but I still couldn't see.
Also, did anyone actually vote for Donald Trump because it doesn't seem like anyone did to me.
Thank God for air-conditioning.
We're all different but the same,
coming from the same place.
America, what have you done to me?
America, the land of the free.
America, what have you done to me?
America, where everyone treated me so beautifully.

Austin was awesome, and probably my favourite city so far—very new, full of musical influence, and progressive. I went busking down on one of the main streets for my Friday

night. It was fun performing for people, chatting and generally just getting to jam, share my music, and try and make a little difference financially.

By this point I had finally found someone to give my bag and gear to after searching and trying. To be honest, the whole affair was a bit anticlimactic. I'd reached out to the Austin Climbing Facebook group and wrote a post that I was willing to give this gear away to a stranger that needed it. I was hoping for someone with some crazy adventure planned to approach me for the gear—and that without it there was no adventure. I kind of fancied that the universe had provided perfect, almost life-changing timing with me giving it away. No such luck. I only had one response; this local young woman who came around to Chris's to pick up the gear. We had a two-minute chat, just a quick thank you and hug … and then off she went to never be heard from again.

I'd asked her to pass it on if she ever ended up not using it. Who knows where it is now, maybe it has climbed some mystical mountain, passing through sherpas and different travellers … or maybe it's still in her closet.

I also was leaving Austin the next day, and had already put all the extra clothes and stuff in a bag that Chris was going to take down to a salvation army charity shop.

I loved meeting and hanging out with people who I'd never met, but I'd also been a lot on my own just to listening to music, or having a coffee or a few drinks. It's hard not to feel creepy sitting there on your own, but it's amazing the connections and people that you meet when you sit alone. I did the same in Austin and it was always a laugh seeing what people knew … which was usually very little.

I would usually find myself explaining that New Zealand is famous for Lord of The Rings. They also knew about the gorgeous scenery, but most people barely knew where it is in the world, or the fact there are two islands rather than one. I learnt more about New Zealand while trying to teach people about it while travelling and I quickly realised that I didn't know that much before I left!

I'd been trying very hard to make it up to Utah to go paragliding. I was so keen on that, but me being me … I had only just checked my itinerary and realised I was flying out a week earlier than I'd been telling everyone. So back to Pennsylvania it would be, to pick up my basketball chair, then I'd be off for a week in New York to experience the Big Apple.

I was going to hitchhike from Austin back to the east coast and test out the hammock I had bought, but then as a last thought before falling asleep I decided to book a train to leave in the morning, mainly because it was the easier option. So I booked a forty-nine-hour train ticket back to the east coast via Chicago. So random. I was running out of time and didn't want to miss my flight over to Europe.

The train ride might have been long, but unlike on a plane, I can use my chair to get to the toilets—which is always my main worry while travelling because of the peeing thing.

I had to switch trains at Chicago, and with a bit of time to burn I went to have a look at the buildings. I remember looking out the windows along the way how the landscape had changed from the leafless trees that had greeted me when I arrived in winter; now it was spring, and we were surrounded by hills full of green.

It was fun coming back to Priscilla, staying there as her guest, not having to work for a place to stay like last time. It was fitting that this was the place I came back to, coming full circle and being able to talk to Priscilla about my adventures over the last couple of months. It was like returning to the mothership.

When I'd arrived just months before, I was lost, trying to figure out how to adjust to the fallout after my dreams of getting a van and playing basketball around the country hadn't worked out. She was the first person to accept me on the Workaway programme, and gave me that chance. I ended up basing most of my travels around that, so I owe her so much.

More consequentially, I owe her my gratitude for the idea to do my blog and, eventually, this book. She was an adventurer herself, having once biked right across America, and this gave me some inspiration.

When I arrived at Priscilla's the first time, I was off grid, and she had suggested I do a blog to chronicle my journey and to engage people around the world as I went. It wasn't much of a stretch for me; I was keeping a journal anyway, so blogging was like a journal but for the whole world to see, and not just in my rugged little pocket journal.

So by the time I made it back to her, I'd been blogging for two months, something I'm grateful for, because it allowed me not just to freeze my memories in time, but to share them with others, including you.

I spent a couple of nights with Priscilla at the church, picked up my basketball chair and caught a train up to New York—the last stop.

| *New York, New York*

NEW YORK WAS HOW I THOUGHT IT WOULD BE: busy, with much to see and do. I did a lot of pushing around the city, and the hostel I stayed in was full of wonderfully friendly people and staff, but outside, I discovered that things were different. New Yorkers were just as you saw them on the movies; driven, perpetually on a mission, almost … ruthless. I cruised around the city, having coffees and lying in parks, trying to break down the locals' barriers.

I quickly discovered that a week in a place like New York isn't enough time to infiltrate people's bubbles. Most of the time, my natural friendliness was met with little more than blank stares.

I had a strange encounter one night, though, while wheeling around aimlessly. By this point I couldn't afford to eat out or drink out. I stumbled upon this rooftop bar on Google Maps and was intrigued; I'd never been to one.

So I found my way to the building—at least, I thought it was the building. I wheeled up to the door of this grand-looking hotel in the middle of the city, and standing there was a doorman, dressed in a smart uniform. I asked him if this was the right place. He nodded politely. "Yes, sir; come with me."

I wasn't about to say no. He led me into the elevator and then, oddly, took me for this private tour of one of the empty floors that is usually a night club. Super random and strange, as it was just me and this giant of a bouncer in a huge empty club that looked like the kind of penthouse suite you might see in a rap video, with millionaires partying, girls dancing and champagne flowing.

After the tour he took me up to the rooftop where there was a cute bar, crowded with New Yorkers all dressed up for after-work drinks. And there I was, shabbily dressed in my one and only set of clothes that I was now travelling in.

If I'd had the money, I'd have had a martini. Instead, I sat alone at the bar for 15 minutes, drinking water and trying to invite strangers with my eyes to come and spin a yarn with me. No one was too keen for a chat and I won't force one. So I made my way back to the hostel

Times Square, naturally

eventually, wheeling across the Brooklyn Bridge around midnight.

Another day, I found another rehabilitation hospital after exploring Central Park. As I often did, I felt the urge to go in and offer to chat with the clients who were now adjusting to a new situation in which they weren't as mobile as before. Looking at the place, I didn't get the impression that people could just walk in off the street, but I did anyway. I went up a couple of floors in the elevator, where I spotted some people who were rolling around the halls in their new wheelchair. But didn't see anyone I thought I could approach, so I tried not to look like a weirdo and awkwardly left.

I did have one romantic adventure—or misadventure, you could more rightly call it—which was cringeworthy at the time, but which, looking back, was just one of those mini-disasters that define your youth, and makes a hell of a good story to tell at a bar when you're older.

It began as a Tinder date. Although I'd mainly been using Tinder to just hang out with people while passing through, to have a friend for a day or two, like Mary in Brighton, there were a couple of times that these ended up differently. This was one of those times.

I matched with a young woman—let's call her Carrie, a cute Brooklyn girl with curly black hair. We went for drinks at a bar down the road from the hostel, where we had a laugh and swapped stories.

We wound up sitting outside the hostel, feeling a bit smitten, thanks to immediate chemistry and a drink or two. We kissed awhile, and eventually I invited her into the hostel. Anyone who has stayed in a hostel knows exactly what it is like in those shared rooms: anything goes.

Let's just say that at first, we had the room to ourselves … and then one of the staff came in, showing a new resident to his corner of the room. I felt sorry for him. I'd been on the receiving end of that awkward experience during many a hostel stay, and knew how bad it felt to be the third wheel. So Carrie and I snuck down to the basement, where the common room was. It was 10.00 p.m. and the sign on the door said CLOSED, but an unlocked door is an open invitation, and I guess we both felt reckless.

We were sitting on the make-out couch in the dark, helping it live up to its name, when a staff member came stomping in, switched on the lights, and informed us that not only was the room closed, but that the security cameras were still running, and we were putting on quite a show. Safe to say we said goodbye to each other outside and went on with our separate life adventures. I was flying out the next day anyway, so it wasn't one of

those love stories in which I cancelled my flight for the sake of true love and lived happily ever after in Brooklyn

Bottom line: New York would have been perfect if I'd known someone to show me around or take me to the true local spots, as opposed to the tourist traps. And without money to even go to the tourist attractions, it turned out to be just a lot of wheeling around the city and seeing some of the free or inexpensive sights.

Then it was off to the airport to board the plane to Spain, say goodbye to America and meet up with Julie to travel around Europe.

America, I learnt to let go of the things I thought I needed but didn't, to not judge, and to be open to everyone. I pushed myself further into situations where I had no control, and, more importantly, I learned to start flowing with wherever it was I was going. This is why I came travelling, so thank you.

Wall graffiti in Austin

POSTCARDS FROM EUROPE

I ARRIVED AT JFK airport fourteen hours too early to make my way over to Europe after misreading my flights as departing at 11.00 A.M. instead of 11.00 P.M.... but I guess it was better to be fourteen hours too early than fourteen hours too late!

I didn't really want to Uber back to Brooklyn either, so I spent the day drifting between napping on those not-so-comfortable airport seats and indulging in some people-watching, not knowing that ultimately I'd find myself in four weeks' time sitting in the boot of a rental car, in Norway, drinking a Norwegian dark beer and looking out at the beautiful fjords, making up my mind that it was time to go back to New Zealand and check back into reality.

My friend Josh had asked me to be the best man at his wedding, which still five months away, but when it came to wedding plans, time grows wings. More urgently, the New Zealand basketball team was planning a trip to

China for the world championship qualifiers in October, the athlete in me was whispering into my ear, reminding wanderer me that it would soon be time to head home and start training.

Where There Was One, Now There Were Two

Barcelona, Spain

I WAS A BIT NERVOUS, as I was going to meet up with Julie in Spain. I'd met her on the dancefloor some time before, back in New Zealand, on a night when I was checking out the town on my own. It was two weeks before the lease was up on my apartment, and my big plan was to live in my car for the next year, to save money for my trip. I'd planned to use the showers at a campsite and then just store my stuff at a friend's house. I kind of liked the idea of being able to change what I was looking at each day, and I spent pretty much the whole day at work anyway. There was nothing going to stop me making this trip happen … if I had to sleep in my car for a year, I would.

But to help me out, Julie offered me a room free of rent. It was hard to say no, even though I was looking forward to spending that time on my own. So I took her up on it, and it wasn't long until we shared a room, and even though we both knew I was heading away for an undefined amount of time, it seemed to work.

Most of my anxiety came from knowing what I was like when travelling with people … not so good. I'm a bit of a free spirit and struggle when I have to tone down the 'freeness' of my decisions.

Anyway, off to Spain—my last planned destination. I hadn't booked anything after this—no tickets home, no tickets onwards. By this time I'd taken a huge gulp of freedom and decided I liked the taste. Would I be able to adjust to the limitations of exploring in tandem on the final leg of my journey?

As soon as I landed in Spain, I went straight off to the hotel to meet up with Julie. She had flown over from New Zealand, expecting an adventure of her own, as she'd never backpacked before.

We spent the week in the heat of Barcelona, wandering the beautiful streets and markets adjusting to long periods in each other's company … or, at least, I was the one doing the adjusting. We picked up a smattering of Spanish along the way. I got to a stage where I could say what I needed to, which was especially handy when trying to catch a train up to Jaca, a small town up in the Pyrenees near the border with France.

The trains weren't level with the platform, so I needed a wheelchair lift to get in. But as I found out, it was easier to say I was okay and just jump in and then jump off, with Julie lifting my chair in and out, as some of the stations didn't have lifts and the language barrier made it hard to communicate that I would be fine at the stations without them.

We'd assumed that the cheaper the accommodation, the more likely we were to end up in a local type of area instead of a tourist hub, and we were right. There were no tourists to be seen—not counting us, that is—and the place we stayed in was in the heart of town, surrounded by crooked little streets and narrow buildings. Also, it was my preferred option because after six months on my own, I was practically skint.

I loved Spain. The language wasn't too hard to pick up, and the trains were cheap. From Jaca we trained up to San Sebastian. Although San Sebastian and Barcelona are major cities, I was determined to keep off the main tourist paths and experience the real culture of the countries. Julie and I would just show up at the train station that day and book our ticket to wherever we needed to go and then book our accommodation while on the train.

You're an Inspiration

Bordeaux, France

AFTER A SHORT TRAIN TRIP, we were in a completely different country, speaking a totally different language. That amazed me; after all the effort I put into learning as much Spanish as I could, it meant nothing now that I was in France. I loved the elegance of the language and it was beautiful to listen to, but decided to let the phone do the work for this one—I knew I'd only be in France a week or so.

We went first to Bordeaux. Again, we let the way of the wanderer pick where we were going to spend the night. Deciding on a whim whether it 'felt like us'. After changing my Workaway profile to have Julie on it as well, we heard back from Andy, who was in Marmande in the south-west, and willing to have us come work.

Andy took us to a big, beautiful French farmhouse in the countryside. I'd assumed Andy was French, but when he turned up to pick us up, he opened with some cheeky joke in his English accent ...now, that was a surprise! We spent the week there cutting bamboo (for what, he never told us), making music, and enjoying the jokes from our English host (who didn't speak a word of French, which was pretty hilarious) and the food from the local French towns.

Conquering bamboo

Part of what Andy wanted was inspiration for his music, and what he did was write songs with his Workawayers. It was amazing that Simon, a Kiwi guy from Nelson, was also doing Workaway and showed up a day after we got there. I had only run into a couple of Kiwis the whole time I'd been travelling.

The week passed, and, as relaxing as it was, it was time to move on. As we said our goodbyes, Simon said something that got me thinking. I'd heard these words quite a lot, especially during the six to seven months I was solo travelling. "You're an inspiration," he said. I guess I never really took it in before, trying to take what people had said in the context in which they saw it.

Simon seemed like a hearty Kiwi bloke, so for some reason when he said it, something stuck. I had to step outside of myself to see the views of people saying it, because to me (and I think to anyone else that has been "inspiration"), the goal wasn't to inspire.

Mine was more selfish than that: I just wanted to find myself, and this seemed like the path I should go down. Well, why not inspire? On reflection, I realised that you didn't need to climb Mount Everest to inspire; inspiration was a friendly smile from an unlikely character, or a conversation with a man you thought was homeless but actually chose to be there, because he himself was once inspired.

Inspiration starts with a smile, a smile towards the person least expecting it.
From my journal.

Your Instincts are Smarter Than You
Zurich, Switzerland
11 June 2017

WE HAD HEARD BACK FROM A WORKAWAY HOST in Switzerland, and that was perfect because I wanted to catch up with a friend from back home who was living there. Back on the train we went, from Bordeaux to Switzerland via Paris. And although we didn't see much of anything on the cab ride between the two train stations in Paris, I could get a sense of the grandness of the legendary city and the amazing history behind it. I always find there's a lot to do in the grand cities like London, New York and Paris, but I'm always in a hurry to leave them. I just couldn't wait to go see the people of the small towns and hear their stories, lie in the fields and watch life buzzing around me.

Not having pre-planned trips or buying the tourist train tickets means that you can end up on the wrong train. And there were numerous times where I rushed to jump on a train that was leaving, then had that feeling of 'wait a second, this doesn't feel right' and then jumped back off instantly as it was about to take off. That happened a lot on the way from France into Zurich, meaning we arrived at 2.00 A.M.

Although it could have been solved by sitting and planning the multiple train trips or buying a tourist ticket … where is the fun in that? Also, it was nice to see Zurich at that hour, when all was quiet.

One thing I've learnt is to trust your instincts. The subconscious is a powerful thing, and your hunch doesn't have to make sense as long as it feels right in your gut. There are times to think, and then there are times to trust what your heart has to say. While I'm travelling, the majority of my direction and decisions are made with my heart. Problems are created and solved with the mind; the heart just follows the path it's meant to follow.

Every bit of knowledge I've gained has been a lesson, and before I carry on with being in Zurich at two in the morning, let me tell you about a small experience that has stuck with me, a lesson that made me who I am now and influenced how I approach things.

I was around eighteen when I started playing tennis, wheelchair tennis. It's hard to imagine how we move around the court with the racket, quick enough to hit the ball in a chair, I know. I got to a high level, anyway.

I was focused. I made number one in the New Zealand men's rankings, number six in the world for the junior rankings and around seventieth in the men's rankings.

One particular time stood out. I'd trained like crazy, but had one season where I just couldn't get into a rhythm and was not performing well in any of the tournaments. I was trying so hard to think about what I was doing, what I'd been practicing. It was frustrating. My timing was out and I wasn't playing like I'd trained at all, up until the last match of my season. It was the World Team Cup in Turkey and I was in the number one seed position for the NZ team, so I had to face all the number one players from the countries we played. And although I could play well, I was a level below those guys. I didn't have the same training resources or the money to travel to all the tournaments that those guys did.

I was facing a player from the USA. He was good. And with the way my lead-up tournaments had been going, I really had to step outside myself and come back as a different person to achieve what I believed I could. We had sports psychologists, nutritionists and fitness gurus, so I knew how to be professional, how to take myself into the present moment and how to work out my brain to win.

It was a beautiful day. We were playing on clay courts, and I'd always go out before the match with my headphones on and go over my plan and start the intense focus, and concentrate all my will and energy into total belief of myself. This day was a little different, though. It was my last match of the season and my toughest opponent, and I was meant to be in my peak rhythm— but wasn't.

So five minutes before my match, I sat with my eyes closed and brought myself more into the present moment than I ever have. Everything felt like it was in slo-mo, and that minute or two felt like it was endless as I breathed in and tried to feel all the energy around me and in me. I completely let go of my mind. There was no past or future. I filled my heart with desire, with the absoluteness of possibility. I held this focus for the two hours or so that the match lasted. I fought, hustled, believed and focused on the present moment with intensity … and lost.

However, I played at a level higher than my training and lead-up performance had made me capable of. The coach of the other player came up afterwards and told me that I was the first person to challenge him in the World Team Cup tournament.

I knew that with enough of the right training, hard work and focus, I could beat whoever I came up against, but in this situation I hadn't had enough of the right training or overseas competition. However, this match taught me to trust my instincts, fill my heart with a fire, and that in the present moment you are capable of a lot more than you had thought. I now spend a lot of time trusting my heart and being in the present moment … and that will be one of my great lessons.

| *Freefalling into Freedom*

Mettmenstetten, Switzerland

12 June 2017

FROM ZURICH, Julie and I made our way to the small town of Mettmenstetten … beautiful. We met Maja and her husband, Christian, who spoke good English. I loved our Workaway there. We spent our work time baking bread in the solar oven, going for massive rides (me in my chair and the others on their bikes)—the longest being something like thirty kilometres to go pick up some strawberries for Maja's homemade jam—and looking after the cats. It was lovely, and they were hardcase, having cycled all over the world doing thousands of kilometres at a time. It sounded perfect: seeing the country by bike. I desperately tried to find a handcycle to use so Julie and I could go on a weeklong bike ride and freedom camp along the way. Switzerland was made for cycles and everyone cycled everywhere.

In pursuit of strawberries

Although I didn't end up finding a handcycle, we still did our long daily trips to visit people, and at one stage we went up to Maja's father's birthday celebration at their home in the hills. That was a beautiful push, but, my gosh, it was a long, steep hill on a hot day. I love that stuff—hard, though.

We caught trains all over the place, cycled to different towns around Switzerland, and went for swims in some of the many lakes that dotted the landscape. I'd organised to go visit Josh, a close friend from high school—not the Josh who was soon to marry Ayla with me as his best man, but a friend all the same. He was up in Kandersteg, and along the way we hopped on and off the train in some of the towns we passed through, because it was amazingly easy do so. Everything was so accessible.

We decided to stop off in Interlaken for a couple of nights—our first night in a hostel since leaving Barcelona. The fairy tale town was full of life, the perfect place if you wanted to do something crazy like skydiving, bungy jumping … pretty much anything where you jumped off something.

Jezza, a friend from back in NZ, had been hooking me up with contacts along the way. He is a tetraplegic who has also done a lot of travelling and had made contacts all over the world. He gave me a couple of people to go talk to about doing something crazy.

So I went to the AlpinRaft, one of those crazy adventure places. I thought that since I hadn't done a bungy or anything, f%$k it, I'd give that a crack. They were more than willing to let me flop out of the gondola, even though they'd never had a paraplegic do a bungy before. Also, amazingly, they were all Kiwis apart from one guy, and that may have helped with the 'she'll be right' attitude.

As I said before, I'd always been a bit nervous about doing things that made me look disabled or out of control of my body, but since I'd been travelling, I'd loosened up and I found if I just said yes, the rest was downhill from there. So up in a group we went, up and up in the gondola just outside of Interlaken. It was a beautiful sight over the lake.

I was last—everyone had done their jump. It was funny (and maybe a bit unnerving) hearing the few seconds after someone's jump—silence and then 'ahhhhh' screams. It was my turn to go up to the ledge. I jumped out of my chair and sat on the edge, looking down, and I was thinking about the awesome pose I was going to do when I pushed myself off and turned to the camera on the way down. So let me tell you, as soon as I left the ledge, I completely forgot about the pose and I was just in survival mode after that—not that I could do anything else, even if I'd wanted to.

Once I was back safely in the gondola, rather than dangling just feet from the lake water, I felt a surge of emotion. Part of it was relief that I didn't die, and the other part was a mixture of adrenaline-fueled energy and happiness. I can see how people get addicted to the feeling. As the gondola sailed back down to terra firma, everyone was too filled with the same feeling to acknowledge that there was a person in a wheelchair in the gondola, and that was cool with me.

I'd never felt that feeling before, having the choice to step over that ledge, but once I had let go, there was nothing I could do ... I was freefalling. Nothing was in my control. I didn't have time to adapt, to breathe, to enjoy the fall, or even to process what was going on until afterwards. I still vividly remember the feeling of freefalling and the feeling of feeling something new after my 28 years so far and trying to process it where it should be stored ... stored in the fear, happiness or excitement category in my brain.

That night, after the bungy, we decided that we would freedom camp, so we had dinner and waited until dark, because we weren't sure if you were really allowed to freedom camp around there. But once it was dark, we snuck into the bushes by the lake and set up the hammocks. At this time I feel the need to point out that getting into a hammock in a chair, even in daylight, has its challenges. I have to transfer myself by pushing up with one hand on my wheelchair and one hand on whatever I'm transferring too—in this case, a wildly swinging hammock. Can you picture how sketchy that is in the dark? Also, sleeping out in nature wasn't as comforting as I'd have thought. I felt like I was at the perfect height for a wild animal to come and taste a bit of human, or for a snake or other equally ghastly creepy crawly to slither down from the tree. So I can tell you, for someone that isn't Bear Grylls that the sleep wasn't the magical one-with-nature sleep you'd expect.

The next morning it was an early rise because we didn't want to get caught. Good thing, because we woke up to the most glorious sunrise over the lake and mountains. We topped it off with a dip in the lake under the gentle colours of the lightening sky ... and rinsed some clothes while we were at it.

Friends are Worth the Time

Kandersteg, Switzerland

23 June 2017

NOW TO MAKE OUR WAY UP TO KANDERSTEG. That was one of those 'catch a bunch of trains and make sure we get off and on at the right stop' trips.

We made it up to this beautiful little village in the mountains and caught up with Josh, one of my close circle of friends who I grew up with during and after high school. He'd left to live in Switzerland a year or so before. Since I was always on the move, we really didn't have much time, which was crazy, because there we were, together on the other side of the world about to have a coffee! But he had to go back to work and I had to make my way back to do the housesitting for Christian and Maja. I left the coffee shop feeling buoyant and cheerful. It was so nice to see a face from home in another country.

If I'd been on my own, I'd have stayed with Josh. Friends are everything and we were on the other side of the world together. I looked at this beautiful village in the mountains, and felt sad that I felt like I couldn't just wing it and tell Josh. "Looks like I'll be staying a few nights with you then." Not because Julie couldn't handle winging it—we'd literally snuck into the bushes a couple

of nights before to put up our hammocks by the lake! I loved how that 'no' was also not part of her vocabulary. But she was here on her own adventure, and it didn't feel right to make her feel stalled.

| *Naked Culture Shock*

Copenhagen, Denmark

27th June 2017

WE BOOKED A FLIGHT TO COPENHAGEN, where I'd organised for us to stay with Elsabeth in a commune. I'd met Elsabeth in Louisiana, and she'd told me it cost something like fifty euros for the week to stay where she lived, so you couldn't argue with that.

It turned out to be small and rustic, with charming cabins and lots of greenery all around. The houses were so close together that a tall person could almost lie down in the driveway and have his hands and feet touch opposite doors! It looked like something you might stumble across in the woods somewhere.

The culture seemed a little more open in Europe, and it suited me. People were less worried about the things that didn't matter. Everyone was out talking to each other, or playing music together. The wonderfully strange part was that it lay in the heart of Copenhagen, and it felt like you were in Hand Christian Anderson territory until you stepped from the driveway to a main road.

Despite the hippy feel, I didn't pick up on any kind of philosophy or belief system; it just felt like an amplified European culture. Everyone was allowed to do as they saw fit, and let everyone else be. Maybe that's why some of the Scandinavian countries are the happiest.

When we first arrived, we weren't quite sure what to expect from this commune. Take the shared unisex showers, for example. For the first few times I tried to go when I knew no one was there, but I got caught out once or twice. It was a shock sitting there on a stool butt naked in this big open room with shower heads coming down from the ceiling, men and woman coming in like it just was no big deal, but it was quite nice getting over

that whole nudity thing. There was nothing weird or perverted about it like it would be back home.

We spent our days in Copenhagen wandering around the city. Although there were a lot of apartment-style buildings, there was something quiet and peaceful about it.

The Wrong Way is Sometimes The Right Way

Copenhagen to Sweden

ONE THING I LOVE TO DO in places I have never been is to just jump on a bus or a train and see where I end up. I very rarely look at a map to get a total layout of the country, state or city. My favourite places have been ones where I just stopped when it felt right. One day in Copenhagen, Julie and I decided to explore separately. I bought a train pass and just got on, getting off at the last stop about forty minutes out of the city.

I wheeled around and took it in—not that there was much to see … until I got down to this little wharf on

the water after pushing up a dirt track and through some bush. I was delighted—and deeply moved. This was what I'd been searching for. I'd left my life behind so I could find places just like this, places to re-energise, to stop for a while and just *be*.

Another day, Julie and I decided to head out to see more of Copenhagen, but caught the train going the wrong direction. Five minutes later we were in Sweden, without our passports and having to tell the passport control guys that we'd just caught the train the wrong way and would hop straight back on back to Denmark. Running afoul of immigration officials isn't what any traveller looks forward to. Surprisingly, they believed us; it was nice getting believed on your word. They didn't escort us anywhere either. They just told us in a neutral kind of way to get back on the train back. Whew!

A week in one place seemed like the perfect amount of time. Any longer and the feeling of needing to move on started creeping in. So, after a week, we went and picked up the rental, put the portable hand controls in and started driving, with no intention of booking accommodation because we were sitting in it.

So back across the bridge from Denmark to Sweden we went—on purpose this time. We just got on the right road … and drove.

| *Two Weeks in the Smallest Mobile Home*
Öland, Sweden

THE CAR WE RENTED was a small hatchback, long enough for me to stretch out in with the seats folded down, but just a little bit too short for Julie. We were loaded up with our bags, my chair (I had left my basketball chair in the hotel storage in Spain at the start of the Europe trip) and a couple of cushions that we'd bought for pillows … because we were in luxury mode now.

We drove north along the east coast of Sweden with the intention of going inland at some point to start making our way to Norway. Looking at the GPS, we

decided to catch a ferry across to a small island, Gotland, before we started west. We ended up in a cute seaside village and parked up to get comfortable for the night.

Then I changed my mind, figuring that it was too early to stop driving, so we drove all the way to Öland, where we could catch the ferry in the morning. We parked in a clearing in a bike park next to the ocean, arriving just in time to catch the beautiful horizon, with the sun saying goodbye for the day.

| *A Hard Decision*

Jönköping, Sweden

3 July 2017

I WOKE UP AFTER A BEAUTIFUL NIGHT'S SLEEP, even though it was the boot of the rental car. I imagine it was from the legit cannabis oil someone in the commune had given me, which is meant to calm things like spasms and pain. Now, medicinal cannabis oil doesn't have the

THC (well, the not this one anyway), which means it doesn't have the chemical that gets you high.

Deciding not to catch a ferry to Gotland meant it ended up being a big day of driving—right across Sweden. We only stopped only around midway for lunch at a lakeside city called Jönköping.

While driving towards the border of Norway, we caught the sunset, which was beautiful as it spilled down over the slowly spinning sails of the windmills, and pulled atop a hill to appreciate the last of the Swedish landscape.

It wasn't always sweetness and light, though; travelling rarely is. We tried to find somewhere near the southern coast to sleep as the sun went down, but no such luck. We ended up getting lost along some private land along the way and driving down country roads in the dark. At around midnight we finally found a place where we could back up against a lake just off the road.

Sweden into Norway

4 July 2017

RISING EARLY TO CROSS THE NORWEGIAN BORDER, we noticed subtle differences between how they do things in Sweden as compared to Norway. For the most part, there were just little things; for example, the road markings slightly changed; barriers on the side of

the road were different, and street signs changed slightly in style and language. It was a brand new day, and we were in a new country.

Avoiding the big city of Oslo, we headed up into the mountains, through magical tunnels and over bridges that dwarfed any car passing them and onwards through the fjords until four in the afternoon. We pulled over next to a beautiful lake, opened up the boot, cracked a beer and played the guitar to soothe our souls for the day.

We'd bought the beers the day before, just in time, as the country had an alcohol curfew. Technically, we were breaking the law, as we weren't allowed to drink in public. But since we were the only two living beings in the vicinity, we figured we had a good get out of jail free card.

Personally, I think Norway is onto it with their alcohol laws; you can't buy alcohol after 6.00 p.m. and you can't buy it from just any old store—and we were always in the middle of nowhere. It's probably another reason for their happiness—no one is hungover.

It was lovely being in a place where there weren't many people, surrounded by a beautiful landscape … it reminded me of home … home … some heavy thoughts that had been working my way into my mind since I arrived in Europe reappeared as I sat there, taking in this beautiful Scandinavian landscape, looking at it all with a kind of longing to run into the forests and forcibly continue my pilgrimage instead of having problems of reality of home on my mind.

We were getting tired, and the close confines and uninterrupted togetherness began to take its toll. Julie and I began having little arguments. Pressure was building up, especially since I'd all but run out of money and knew I'd have to start looking at working again. My reality check wasn't far off.

After arriving in Bergen, we booked our tickets home in a couple of weeks' time. The part of me that is an athlete was loud in my ear, telling the part that is a wanderer that it was time to head home and start training. There was no way that I'd be going to China unfit for the world championship qualifiers.

Although I'd done so much, achieved so much, and learned so much about myself and the world, I couldn't shake the nagging feeling that I was cutting my adventure short. The idea of returning home felt like failure. I had told everyone that they might not see me for a long time— and yet, just nine months later, I'd be back, tanned, well-travelled but broke.

As I booked my flights, I kept reassuring myself that it was okay, that I wouldn't get too involved with anything when I flew back. Just train, play my part at Josh's wedding, and earn some money. Then I planned on being back on the road again, a dishevelled but loveable vagabond. The lure of the road was too sweet.

I'd seen so many different cultures, and now there was a fire kindling inside me to not just pass through these places, but to set up and live there. Travelling like this had been amazing, and I was confident in the fact that I'd proved to myself that the wheelchair was no barrier when it came to travelling … but I was missing something. Like being in New York and not being able to infiltrate the culture or people's bubbles; I'd been just an outsider passing through. I was coming to realize that the journey wasn't just a physical movement from place to place but the interactions and experiences with the new people around me.

Something that I was lacking in this European trip. When I'd been travelling solo, I'd struck up conversations with strangers wherever I went, but the thing about travelling in pairs is that you tend to not to put yourself out there with strangers as much. They, in turn, are less likely to try to penetrate *your* bubble. I realised I wasn't putting myself out into social situations as much, and just having shared experiences with Julie.

I felt nervous at the thought of flying home, scared that I would get stuck in the grind and forget that this was what I wanted. Scared that it was a mistake to go home early, but a hard decision had to be made.

I Might Not Have Limits, But My Wheelchair Does

Bergen, Norway

7 July 2017

A COUPLE OF DAYS chilling in Bergen and it was time to move on from morning coffees in the city. I was really keen to set up somewhere I could maybe do a bit of a hike in the mountains, so we were off driving again. Instead of sticking to the highways, which would get you from one place to the next quickly, we took a route that was only wide enough for one car. There were almost no one else coming in the other direction; everyone had obviously decided to use the motorways. On the few occasions when we met one coming the other way, it was just slow down to walking speed and look for a little bulge in the road that would allow the cars to pass while our wing mirrors pretty much touched. It was worth the trouble, winding through hills, around beautiful green fjords and through small villages, each one built around a beautiful church.

We ended up picking a road, driving about an hour, and then finding ourselves in a line for a ferry. Well, that was the end of the road, and if we wanted to go any further, it was time to catch a ferry. Looking at the

map, we decided to follow our gut feeling, which was to head the other way to get further north. Backtracking is something I'm not a big fan of, but we backtracked and continued north, driving up through a national park that was edged with lacy snow.

We had multiple stops for me to go pee, and there weren't many toilets around, naturally, so the side of the road it was. At one of the many stops we made, and noticing a signboard announcing hiking trails, we picked a beginners' trail nearby, hoping it wouldn't be too difficult to push along.

We headed up a winding back road, which zigzagged around the mountain, paying the twenty kroner road toll, which was just in an honour box on a gate, and then went further up to the start of what seemed to be a track. We parked up for the night at a spot overlooking other mountains and down at the fjord below, with the sheep to keep us company and the sound of rushing water lulling us. Could our spot have been any better?

8 July 2017

AS USUAL, we had a nice sleep in the car. We woke up early, ready to start our hike. We pushed down a grassy hill and then across a bridge … then it became clear that it would be slow going for me and would be stressful with someone waiting for me as I tried to push across this mushy ground or up the grassy hill.

On my own I might have given it a crack, but there would have been a bit of crawling and dragging my chair up things. But all I would be thinking of was Julie waiting for me, so I flagged it and let Julie walk up and check out some of the track while I made my way back up the grassy hill and simply appreciated the mountain right in front of us, kissed by the brisk fresh air: Breathtaking.

Although my wheelchair is my independence, I compare it to trying go out on an excursion with a stroller—now I know all you parents can relate! Now imagine hiking in the mountains with a stroller, I think you would get as far as I did before deciding to ditch it and carry your baby. Not much fun, huh?

| *It's Okay to Explore on Your Own*
Oslo, Norway
9 July 2017

THE NEXT MORNING we had a look at the map, as in a few days' time we'd have to start making out way back to Denmark to drop the rental back off. We decided to start making our way back at the midway point of

Norway to spend a couple of nights in Oslo and then take our time getting back to Denmark, making our way through the mainland this time.

After a full day's driving to end up in Oslo, we booked into a hostel and then headed outdoors to check things out. Oslo felt like a lot of other bustling cities, a place where people come to work and where travellers arrive on their buses, trains, planes.

We didn't mind going off to indulge in our separate interests. She liked to look at the architecture and I just liked to cruise around. So we went our own ways and met back up that night to go to the movies—a luxury. I don't remember what movie it was, but I do remember it was in English. The infomercials and the introduction to the movie stayed with me, though. Two of the staff came onto the stage to wish us all cinema goers a good movie—never seen that before—and there was shampoo commercial with nudity, another reminder that we were in Europe, because I know in New Zealand there would be a giggle or a parent ready to write an heated email to the company. I enjoyed the openness of Europe, and I think it took down a lot of my body image issues by not making the human body a taboo topic.

We went straight from the theatre to the hostel room, which we had to ourselves, to enjoy our new fondness of each other from our day separation.

On the Brink of the Journey Home

Goodbye, Scandinavia. I loved the culture. I can't quite explain how it felt to me. It was like going back in time, but you seemed further ahead culturally. I'm not finished here and will be back.

THE NEXT DAY WOULD BE OUR LAST ON THE ROAD before we caught a flight back to Spain, so we were making a return trip to, in full winding-down mode. We just spent the day taking our time driving, stopping off here and there to stretch the legs or to get a coffee. It was a day of time wasting; nothing spectacular, but nice and relaxing nonetheless. That night we parked in town in a place where the streetlight didn't shine and we hopefully wouldn't get noticed (apart from the fogged-up windows the early runners easily spot in the morning).

The Last Leg: Back to Spain
14 July 2017

WE FLEW INTO FAMILIAR TERRITORY: Barcelona. We were heading home in six days' time, but didn't want to spend those whole six days there, as we had already explored Barcelona when I'd arrived from the States. I loved the vibrancy, but wanted to see where we'd find ourselves if we just jumped on a train.

We ended up in what seemed like a mini Barcelona, Lleida, a city in the Catalonia. It was lovely and full of more local people than tourists. I'd put the wrong date when booking the hotel on the train, so we showed up at the hotel (which was sooo cheap—thirty euros a night) a day early and had to wander down to another one nearby for a room.

I was so fit before I had left, training right up to the end, and now I definitely wasn't. The heat and pushing up the hills didn't mix so well with this unfit body. How does that happen? Travelling on a limited budget, I blame the kindness of the Workawayers, who'd fed me up on scrumptious meals, coffee and a wine here and there.

We mooched around the city, with lots of walking/pushing, bouncing back and forth from the hotel, which was acting like a hub for breaks in between. There were a

few places on the streets heading up the hills where there was only access by steps, so I reversed my chair up and popped down them when I had to. At the top of the hill was a massive cathedral and it was lovely to look over Lleida from there.

After two nights in the city, it was time to catch a train to the end of the line, hoping our mystery destination would be amazing. We ended up in La Pobla de Segur—not so glamorous and certainly not a lot to do that time of year. We booked four nights there, but there are only so many times you can walk up and down the same street, so after two days we were back on the train to Barcelona.

The trip between La Pobla de Segur and Lleida was beautiful, though. In a place that seemed so dry, there were deep green lakes with towering canyons running along the train track.

I'd left my basketball chair at hotel I'd stayed in when I first arrived in Spain, so I had to make sure that was still there—chairs aren't cheap. Ten grand for a chair! Lucky for me, it was still there right where I had left it, in their storage room.

The Journey Ends
20 July 2017

OUR FLIGHT WAS EARLY IN THE MORNING, and instead of booking another night's accommodation, we chose to sleep in the airport. We taxied there and then slept on the floor in the hall with some other travellers.

I was sad to start making my way back. I wasn't quite ready ... not even a little bit ready, actually. I'd run out of money, but I was confident with what I'd learnt travelling on my own that I could survive if I stayed—and I still had my guitar to busk. In fact, I'd say I would have a better time than I would if I had money. I'd be forced to keep putting myself out there. But I knew I had to accept this change. I wanted to go to China with the team, I should

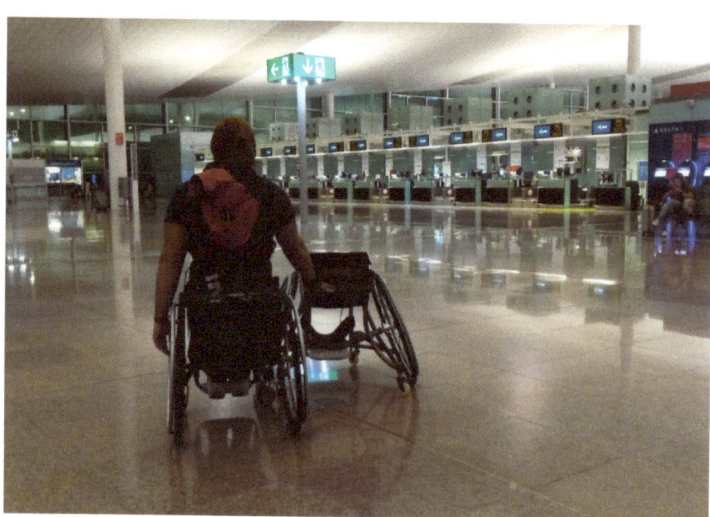

get home a few months early to train. Pushing up those steep hills in Lleida had definitely made that clear.

So that was my decision, because I could keep saying I need to do this and that before I leave and next thing you know I'm forty and still wandering around, unmoored. Now I could go back home, train, get my fitness back, and pay my bills. And then start afresh some day with all the traveling know-how I'd accumulated, like a true wanderer, with the freedom from financial cares.

Catching Some Shut-eye in Hong Kong
Istanbul to Hong Kong

WE HAD A FULL DAY ON LAYOVER IN ISTANBUL, so we caught a train into the city and wandered around before heading back to the airport. It was a very male dominant culture, and going from Europe where all the culture is open and free to a place where people were covered head to toe was a shocker. I didn't get a chance to understand anything, unfortunately; only observed briefly. I left feeling like I needed to spend more than a day in places like this, not just as a passer-by.

Back at the airport, it was a long coffee-fuelled wait—and then we were on the next flight to Hong Kong, where we had a full twenty-two hours, enough time to leave

the airport, explore the underground train system and see how different the city looked lit up.

Instead of sleeping in the airport—again—we found a room online where we could stay for the night. They weren't expecting us, and though it had the feel of a "massage place"—you know what I mean—we still stayed here. It was only one night, and we knew we'd laugh about it later.

We were greeted at the door of this unnamed apartment by a woman in a nightie, who looked slightly confused at what we were doing. Eventually, we showed her the booking and were invited in, but I have a feeling that she was expecting different type of customer. She led us down a hallway lined with small doors. Our tiny room was jam-packed, with barely enough room for a double bed and some air-conditioning units.

It was just like in the movies where you see the guys sweating, fanning themselves and swearing at the aircon in their small apartment—hot and humid; a memorable experience, for sure.

The next day there was a short train ride back to the airport … and then we'd be back on a plane to New Zealand.

HOME TO REFLECT

THE DEFINITION OF "HOME" has now changed for me. Home to some may be the house they grew up in, where their parents still live, or maybe the city where they first lived. But as I sat there reflecting on the last year of my life, I realised I'd learnt how to make any situation my "home" in a short amount of time.

A few times during my journey, people assumed I was homeless (I imagine because of my big beard and general aura of scruffiness), and my response was that I wasn't homeless, I was home-free. Free to make the world my home, to have a home here one day and there the next. While I admit there's a warm feeling of familiarity each time I come back into New Zealand, I revel in this new feeling of freedom, soaking it up.

From the outside it looked like a quiet year slipped by, with only the odd Facebook update or Insta post. It was ironic, because after all that wandering, I'd came home to be completely lost. My search hadn't ended. I was searching for something to fill the gap between now and old age—maybe that's just what happens as you exit your twenties. But when you ask me about my year, I'd say it was filled with kind hearts and loud laughs, new languages and new friends, right vibes and starry nights, music and dancing until 3.00 a.m.

I hadn't told anyone I was coming home, mainly because I had no idea what I was going to do and how long I was going to stay. But in short order, I settled back into my friendships, work and training.

I looked for a place on my own, and found one out in the most raw and beautifully rugged places—Birdlings Flat. I spent that first summer drinking wine, playing music, finishing a draft of 'this book, and watched the sun go down a many a time on the beach.

Nevertheless, the drive remained inside me, the drive to further my taste, learn new lessons and follow the siren call of adventure further down the path I had started.

EPILOGUE ... THREE YEARS ON

"Thousands of candles can be lighted from a single candle, and the life of the candle will not be shortened. Happiness never decreases by being shared." – Buddha

WE'VE COME TO THE END OF MY JOURNEY... *so far*. Thank you for sticking it out with me; I appreciate your company. Here are just a few quick snapshots, the bookend to my story, before we part ways.

Pondering the changes in my life

I have a container full of scrap notes, records of my mind spilling out through the end of a pen. Re-reading through those, I realise how lost I was in my early twenties; I have page after page of me trying to decipher the code of happiness so that I could manifest it in my own life.

Rather than being diaries full of the dark thoughts, they were diaries full of that desperation of code, reminders to myself to project happiness. I guess it worked, because without them, the me of the past, my thoughts, and feelings would be forgotten.

I don't have that desperation to escape to self-exploration anymore, no burning desire to scratch an itch—I travel for knowledge and pleasure now, not out of a desperate need to understand who I am. Happiness found me the same way friends and their children grow old—without you noticing unless you look back.

What do I value?

As it seems to be sneakily passing, I value time. The time that I had to adventure, and find myself when I needed to. The time that I will get to enjoy whatever the future holds.

I value experience, and the fact that I was lucky enough to be able to think something up and then put myself in a position that provided a lifetime's worth of shared and personal experience.

After being away from everyone, family and friends, I value them hugely. I'm grateful to be part of their lives, especially now that I've spent the last few years running around the world.

A Host Rather than a Guest

I went back onto Couchsurfing—but this time, as a host. I understood what it was like to be a wanderer in a strange land, craving a warm bed and hot shower, so it was easy for me to pay the favour forward. My spare room was often filled with travellers with equally amazing stories, some of their journeys just starting and some journeys ending.

Some vibrated with excitement as they went on their way, and others cried as they said goodbye to their adventure and made their way home. Everyone who stayed left an impression on me.

I picked up a wicked Austrian, Dan, straight off the plane ... took him for a sunset beer and then dragged him around town to various live music gigs before we made our way up to a New Year's gathering. Another, a unicycling Frenchman called Alexis, I took to watch my younger sister run her cross-country race. We spent the week learning French and laughing. Dodo the crazy German was my favourite; we rode up hills to watch the sunset and came back down in the moonlight. We spent a few days out on the beach yelling out at the angry ocean.

The list goes on, with crazy stories to be told over a nice cup of tea in a few years' time. If you are wondering whether to host travellers ... do it; what an experience!

Basketball and German Lessons

My wanderlust hadn't diminished, and it wasn't long before the urge to keep moving seized me again. I decided I could kill two birds with one stone—push my basketball to its limits while immersing myself in another culture.

All the best leagues are in Europe—but first I'd have to play in a reputable league down here, and the closest to me was the Australian National Wheelchair Basketball League. A skip through Australia it would be then, before I tried to make it in Europe as an athlete. This gave me a heavy focus and a perfect way to continue to scratch the itch left behind by the travelling bug's bite.

After my season in Australia, it was off to Germany for basketball, language lessons, and the company of ...

Erica

Meeting Erica was one of the more significant changes in my Life After Wandering. We met in July 2018, on the kind of disastrous Tinder date that makes you call your friends afterward and moan. I didn't think that she was interested at all; I made all the conversation and she sat there calmly, not saying too much, not really giving anything away—including signs of interest.

I manfully gave it a second shot, messaging her once I dropped her home, to ask if she wanted to meet again.

Silence.

Next weekend that I got a message from her; as it turned out, mine hadn't got through. She'd waited in vain for me to do something—until her friend forced her to message me, even though she was sure I wasn't interested. A real 21st century scenario; the girl "making the first move". Maybe in a different era we might have never met again, with a communication error like that!

Erica and I started to see each other more and more, even though I was to move to Australia for basketball in six months' time. Our personalities matched so perfectly it just kept evolving. She came over to Australia, stayed with me—and never moved out.

After months in Germany and weeks in quarantine, we began talking about houses, a family and "our" next move. We decided that our next adventures would be together; huge adventures in small Aotearoa—what the Maoris call New Zealand.

Which leads me to …

Corona, Corona

My season in Germany came to an abrupt end with the global chaos brought on by the Covid-19 pandemic. As my Facebook feed filled up with stories of countries going on lockdown, jobs being lost, lives being disrupted while people squabbled over toilet paper, it became clear that my comfortable stint in Munich was about to end.

Germany began to ban gatherings of 1,000 people … then 500 … and then BOOM! The two months that was left of the basketball season were cancelled. Countries began closing their borders, travellers were being sent into quarantine, and the New Zealand government was telling us to come home. The world was starting to look like the opening credits of a post-apocalyptic movie.

Four days after the league came to an abrupt end, Erica and I were stumbling around trying to find flights to Australia before we got locked in for who knows how long, without work, without basketball, without family or friends. We made the hasty but right decision to go home to New Zealand and spend our 14 days' quarantine in our homeland. We booked a flight, even with the risk of it being cancelled as without warning as countries began pulling travel restrictions out of thin air.

I've been saying all through this book that not having a plan was the best way to travel, but the stakes had changed. Trying to go with the flow when the world is locking down is not so easy. As we sat at the airport during a layover in Qatar, extremely thankful that our flight had gone ahead, we looked for an Airbnb to do our quarantine in Christchurch. It was too much to expect our friends and family to take us in when we could very well be infected.

Throughout the 14-hour flight, we cringed as the passenger in front of us drank heavily and hacked and coughed his way across the Tasman Sea. Just a cold … or Corona? Not a pleasant feeling.

Our temporary quarters were a bit expensive, but worth the money, we realized, as our section of the house was self-contained and the property was surrounded by a beautiful garden, where we could walk around and not feel like we were in jail. Throughout our quarantine, we organized jobs and worked on a plan of attack. Where would we live? What would we do? Everything had changed.

A lot of our friends—well, all of them—didn't want to be near us. We almost felt like lepers, which was a bit hurtful, but we understood that everything was unknown, and everyone had a vulnerable family member. We talked to Erica's brother through the window when he came to visit.

A friend, Hannah, was coming in from Europe, and was at a loss for somewhere to do her quarantine. After every imaginable travel mishap, including flight delays and lost luggage, she finally made it, and we welcomed her into our lovely prison.

All around us, more and more measures were being

put in place to prevent the spread of the virus. Schools, shops, entertainment centres began to close. We watched helplessly as the death toll slowly rose, and as the public health system became overwhelmed. But still, we felt lucky that we had a small window in which to learn from the mistakes of other countries, and take action. We sat on anxious tenterhooks, waiting for Erica's Covid-19 test results … days later, they came back negative.

I wheeled across 20 kilometres of Canterbury Plain countryside one hot, beautiful summer's day, risking sunburn, to retrieve my handcycle, knowing that if I didn't have a physical outlet my grumpiness would affect everyone in the house. Yes, I'm thoughtful that way.

The government offered financial help, and we were lucky to have food delivered by friends and family who were willing to come near us. Karen and John dropped off food from their pantry: milk, bread, canned goods and a few treats. They couldn't go shopping, since, even though the nation was told not to panic, and that essential services like petrol stations, doctors and supermarkets would still be open, people were still queuing up at the supermarket to stockpile. It was like Black Friday and Christmas shopping rolled into one.

The days began to blur into each other, full of Netflix and eating, and the occasional ride in the country. Intermittent rain meant we had to spend majority of the time inside, watching TV and playing board games. It was hard having been away for so long, only to be forced to speak to family from a distance, or over the Internet. We lived on the stipend provided by the state, specifically for people who were jobless because of the lockdown. At least I had a regular income coming into my account now.

We watched with hope as New Zealand slowly began to open up, with domestic travel and the possibility of me going back to work being on the cards. Without international travel, there'd be no basketball.

I even spent time reflecting on the most hectic periods in my life, when I figured I'd kill for this amount of free time. My life experiences taught me that, now that I had it, I would be a fool to let it go to waste. I told myself that these weeks of exile in the country were a gift, and not waste a second of them. I used that time to continue learning German. To finish writing this book. To go out on the handcycle at sunset and appreciate the day without having a task to fulfil when I get home or when I woke up the next day. I turned a difficult time of isolation into a blessing. Soon, I knew, I'd be able to visit my friends, and the babies that I hadn't met yet.

When life gives you a pandemic, you seize it as an opportunity to improve yourself ... ever improve yourself.

Remember … life is complicated. It's also simple, and while there are many ways to look at a truth, I believe that truth is singular.

Whatever your beliefs or scientific reasoning, we will, in the bigger picture, all end up in the same place. So treat each other with love. Because it makes sense to.

Peace, and I hope to see you all on the road … Live once, live big.

Much love,
Eamon

www.ingramcontent.com/pod-product-compliance
Lightning Source LLC
Chambersburg PA
CBHW042047290426
44109CB00006B/131